GOD'S GREEN EARTH

MADDIE DUMAS

WESTBOW
PRESS®
A DIVISION OF THOMAS NELSON
& ZONDERVAN

WestBow Press books may be ordered through
booksellers or by contacting:

WestBow Press
A Division of Thomas Nelson & Zondervan
1663 Liberty Drive
Bloomington, IN 47403
www.westbowpress.com
1 (866) 928-1240

ISBN: 978-1-5127-9094-8 (sc)

Print information available on the last page.

WestBow Press rev. date: 6/26/2017

I am the true vine, and my Father is the gardener. · John 15:1 NIV

Contents

Introduction

God placed an idea in my heart. It's been growing for a while, and as I've scattered the concepts on the pages of this book, I have seen the lessons come alive in a way only God can orchestrate. Have you noticed that when you decide you like something, you find it everywhere? I'm right there.

Today, as I got to know a child in the hospital, I asked her what her favorite subject was. She said science. A nurse chimed in and asked what kind of science: Biology? Chemistry? She replied that she liked earth science. The next thing I heard was "like plants". The nurse heard "like planets". He proceeded to ask her if anyone had decided if Pluto was a planet again or not. I thought it was so random, and quickly realized, he misunderstood. So I redirected. "So do you like to grow plants? Or do you just like to learn about them?" She said she wasn't very good at growing them. Then the nurse channeled it back to planets. He was telling her all about an observatory in our area, and she seemed really interested. I was beginning to feel a little embarrassed for him, as our tennis match continued. After the child's procedure was over, I asked if she had said plants or planets. I just wanted to make sure she caught that he had misheard what she said, and wasn't completely nuts.

It was planets.

My mind has been so focused on plants, sowing and growth, that my focus is stuck on this imagery. I wholeheartedly believe God placed this message at my fingertips to share, and I hope I've been faithful and understanding enough to relay the message to those who need to hear it. And I really hope He didn't say planets. So here we go.

Recently, I have come to think of God as a gardener, a masterful Creator, looking at His garden from above. The NIV translation of John 15:1 says, "I am the true vine, and my Father is the gardener". I mostly use the New King James translation of the Bible, so I often read this verse as "My Father is the vinedresser". Either way, God placed this concept at the fingertips of John long before my hands met a laptop. I know His Word is "living and active" (Hebrews 4:12), and He speaks to us now as He did back then. The Bible is full of metaphors and parables relating to gardening, and I do not believe for one second that it is a coincidence. As my good friend, Becky, once told me, "There are no coincidences, only God-instances".

The imagery is everywhere. God points our attention to the lilies. Jesus asks us to consider the sower who leaves seed on three types of soil. He began the world with a garden, and Jesus spent His last night before crucifixion in a garden. If a theme is repeated that many times, I think it benefits us to take a closer look. The Word of God is anything but stale.

I hardly consider myself a gardener, but I can appreciate the beauty of a flowerbed or a sea of bluebonnets. I enjoy a plate of vegetables from our family garden, and I smile each time I pass under the shade of a live oak tree. God has taught me to appreciate Him as our Creator and the Creator of the world. He had purpose behind His design, and I have the glorious job of learning to understand it a little more every day.

To me, this is more than experiencing God's beauty; it's about experiencing His nearness. A seed can do little without a gardener, just like we are helpless without God. My goal in writing this book is for you to cling to God, get a better understanding of His truth through Bible study and prayer, and learn to let Him provide you with what you need.

I truly hope you take what I have to say and use it to deepen your relationship with God. I have absolutely loved learning more about God through my own studies on this topic, and I pray you will too. Plant your garden, let those roots take hold, and ask God to be your Master Gardener. Let Him cultivate your heart to look like His. Enjoy the beauty that will arise from this experience. Prepare for work as you prune and weed, but ultimately, reap the blessings that flow from a life alongside Jesus Christ.

> *"Consider the lilies, how they grow: they neither toil nor spin; and yet I say to you, even Solomon in all his glory was not arrayed like one of these. If then God so clothes the grass, which today is in the field and tomorrow is thrown into the oven, how much more will He clothe you, O you of little faith?"* (Luke 12:27-28)

The Very First Garden

The Lord God planted a garden eastward in Eden, and there He put the man whom He had formed. And out of the ground the Lord God made every tree grow that is pleasant to the sight and good for food. The tree of life was also in the midst of the garden, and the tree of the knowledge of good and evil... Then the Lord God took the man and put him in the Garden of Eden to tend and keep it (Genesis 2:8-9, 15).

Can you see it? Can you just imagine it? The lush, green grass between your toes. Flowers in every color of the rainbow. Huge elephant ears and towering oaks. Vivid red apples and purple grapes. The sun is shining through the canopy of trees, not too bright, not too hot, but just enough to warm your shoulders and illuminate your surroundings. The clouds look like cotton balls, stretched out across the sky. Do you hear the birds sweetly singing? Do you hear a gentle purr of a tiger? (Because tigers were gentle before the fall of man, I am sure.) Does the water taste fresh and cool as you take a sip straight from the stream? You are in the most beautiful garden in all of creation. One look at your environment leads you to worship the Creator. God expressed Himself in the most vibrant way, and placed Adam and Eve right in the middle of it.

The very first command from God to Adam was to "Be fruitful and multiply" (Genesis 1:28). He used a term based on what Adam was surrounded by. How plentiful the Garden must have been to invoke the imagery of filling the earth with offspring! In the meantime, the very first job God gave man was to keep a garden. He had the privilege of not only caring for, but also naming the plants and animals. God created this beautiful landscape, and He wanted to make sure it was maintained. Genesis 2:19-20 tells us, "Out of the ground the Lord God formed every beast of the field and every bird of the air, and brought them to Adam to see what he would call them. And whatever Adam called each living creature, that was its name. So Adam gave names to all cattle, to the birds of the air, and to every beast of the field." The Artist handpicked the gardener.

Naming each flower gave Adam affection for them; it created ownership. God knew it would benefit Adam to be in charge of something because God created us to thrive on success and industry. We see God's intimate knowledge of humankind in the tasks He assigns us, even from the beginning. Every act in Eden had a purpose.

Eden, by definition means "paradise" or "a place of pristine or abundant, natural beauty[1]" I love the exquisiteness that is portrayed by this name. God didn't get better with each geranium and giraffe; He perfected His creation right off the bat. There were no lessons or practice times. He just did it. His work was perfect, pristine. His tendency toward abundance was at our fingertips from the first page of history.

I believe we can see His affection for gardening in the way our Master Gardener introduced Himself. (So, when we think we, as humans, are the most important things on earth, I believe we have to think again. Plus, the flowers don't talk back or kill each other.) It was His way of saying "Good morning, I'm God. I love mankind, beauty in nature, resting on the Sabbath, and calming storms." Obviously, this is my own interpretation, but what an introduction!

Because He knew every detail, God also knew Adam and Eve would ultimately mess up. He knew Adam, unfortunately, would not be in the garden forever, but He set him up for success. He gave them every opportunity to be grateful for the things they had, to appreciate what was around them, and to pursue a life alongside the Maker, rather than a path of selfish ambition. He gave Adam and Eve free will to do what they wanted, and He gave them full disclosure of the only thing they were not allowed to do.

We know how the story ends. Among the punishments that affect us even today, God sent Adam and Eve away from Eden. When I choose punishments for my children, ages five and three right now, I have to choose consequences that will make them sorry they disobeyed. For my older child, it means taking away his tall socks. He decided at age two to wear socks as high as his little knees. That's how the baseball players wear them, after all. If you see him walking around in ankle socks, you can bet he had trouble being obedient. My younger child has been a little more difficult to figure out. His love language is food, and while I know sending him to bed without dinner every so often won't kill him, I know chocolate hits him where it hurts. (He takes after his mama.) I can take away his opportunity for dessert, and he turns into Cinderella running to the fountain (or his bed) to cry.

God knew Adam and Eve would be saddened by the resulting schism from their disobedience, but they wouldn't understand the ramifications in their entirety yet. He did know they would be crushed to leave such a beautiful home.

Notice God didn't completely take away the lovely flowers and trees. He still kept them for His own enjoyment, but he removed Adam and Eve from Eden. I have to imagine there were similar flora elsewhere, but maybe not in such concentration.

I don't know what kind of flowers grew in Eden, but can't you just imagine the scene? How Eve must have longed for the garden when she saw a poppy or a sunflower. Did she feel remorse each time she passed a fig tree? I think God created our minds to remember the good *and* the bad so we could avoid making the same mistakes over and over. It is our duty to look at these times as a way to glorify our God, rather than our shame. He showed the first couple His best work up front. He didn't wait for them to prove their worth. He always acts as if we will make the right choice. What a comforting benefit of the doubt, but also something to strive for. It's hardest for me to know I have disappointed God. Of all the consequences, that's what hits me in the gut every time I sin.

Our Creator, who designed each and every flower, created each fold in our brains. He knows how we tick, and He knows the best way to mold us into Christ followers. He wasn't just acting out of anger when he banished Adam and Eve from the Garden. He had a plan, just like He always does.

I have to assume Heaven will have glimpses of that very first garden. What a sweet aroma we have to look forward to. I don't think for one second it's a coincidence that in Luke 23:43, Jesus tells the thief on the cross, "Assuredly, I say to you, today you will be with Me in Paradise". If you can think back a few pages, we remember, Eden means "paradise". I absolutely love making these connections! Just like God made us in His image (see Genesis 1:27), He made Eden in the image of Heaven. Our Creator designed every petal, every leaf, every blade of grass in Heaven, and then turned around and mimicked it here on earth. (And to think those wildflowers are even more spectacular in Eternity!) I pray to find God written all over creation. When I receive a colorful bouquet from my husband, or the sweetest clover flower from one of my boys, I can look at the intricacy, and trust my Gardener, my God.

God set the tone in the very first book of the Bible. Just like with Adam and Eve, He didn't ask us to earn it‑ He freely gives and shows us what we would miss if we choose to walk away. He showed us what's up His sleeves, and I don't know about you, but it makes me ready to dig in a little more.

2

Planting Seeds

We chose the spot, we dug the hole
We laid the maples in the ground to have and
hold
As Autumn falls to Winters sleep
We pray that somehow in the Spring
The roots grow deep

Planting Trees by Andrew Peterson[2]

If you've ever been on a mission trip, you know very well that sometimes you see the fruits of your labor, and sometimes you don't. You may spend a summer handing out breakfast bars to commuters on the train and never see a single new face at church. You may have a meaningful, God-centered conversation with a single mom living in poverty, and never know if she truly followed God after you leave. You may build a church in another country, and never see the worship services take place. Sometimes God calls us to plant while others cultivate and reap the harvest. And that's okay. Sometimes God plants a few seeds in us, too.

My pastor, John, talks about this a lot when he speaks

of missions. He recounts the story of a trip he took years ago where he saw only seeds. John had an opportunity to return to the site of this mission trip some twenty years later where he got to see the harvest. We aren't always so lucky, but we can rest assured God places gardeners and farmers where the crops need attention.

We are in a great age where we can keep up with a lot of mission fields through social media. I spent a couple of weeks in Greece after my freshman year at Louisiana State University. A friend and I helped a family of missionaries with a few projects, such as interviewing local college students to better understand their religious views, conducting soccer camps with neighborhood children, putting on a carnival, and leading Vacation Bible School with children in a Roma community. We had a day to get acquainted with the community, and then we were in charge of a mission team for the duration of our trip.

I loved seeing the children light up when we arrived to play soccer and volleyball every night. The teenagers who knew a little English explained to us that some of them were from Turkey, Albania, and Georgia, and were not highly regarded among their Greek neighbors. The simple act of socializing with them and including them in a game was huge. I will be the first to tell you, I'm not very athletic, but the girls enjoyed poking a little fun at my volleyball skills (or lack thereof) and teaching me a few tricks. We broke up a few skirmishes, but mostly, it was a wonderful time of fellowship. Our team got to show them they were loved by us, but even more so by God our Father.

The children in the Roma community were a little harder to communicate with, but I can still remember the smiles on their faces when we sang "Hallelu Hallelu Hallelu Hallelujah, Praise ye the Lord" (in Greek, of course). We gave them the name of Jesus and presented the Gospel through Vacation Bible School material.

Our interviews with the college students allowed the missionary family to see what they were working with. Understanding the religious beliefs of the students helped them figure out the best ways to build rapport and present the Gospel in a way that made the most sense.

While we were unable to see a lot of decisions made for Christ in the ten days we were "planting", I have been able to follow the ministry through an email list. I feel fortunate because I can receive updates of people who are choosing to follow Christ. In the beginning, I recognized a few names; now they are strangers, but no less important. It's like they're sending pictures of the garden we planted ten years ago.

During my freshman and sophomore spring breaks at LSU, I also visited Allende, Mexico. Following up the second year was a lot of fun, because I was able to visit familiar faces and names. I felt like our team was welcomed back as family; and we were truly brothers and sisters in Christ. Facebook has allowed me to keep in touch with the pastor of the church. I love seeing pictures of the church building we painted and seeing updates every now and then. More than anything, I love seeing pictures of a room full of people with hearts for God. I can almost hear their beautiful voices being lifted up to Him.

God used these opportunities to plant seeds in my heart as well. In Greece, I went to an international church service where many cultures, languages, and denominations came together with a common thread: Jesus Christ. They worshiped with hands raised and voices high. There was no timidity or feeling like they couldn't sing too loud. They belted it out! I had never seen anything like it, but I loved every minute! My mission partner, Bethany, mentioned to their worship leader that I led worship at our church back home, so I was even given the opportunity to lead the church in "I Could Sing of Your Love Forever". Having led worship with my husband, Daniel, for many years now, I can tell you, this doesn't happen in most churches. Songs are chosen ahead of time to match the sermon or fit a certain template. This isn't to say they are any less worshipful, but we tend to be very formal in our worship service orders. In Greece, a basket of instruments was passed around for anyone and everyone to participate. In the States, we get nervous about a tambourine!

God taught me a lot about worship on that trip. I learned to be less timid. Timidity is not from God, after all (2 Timothy 1:7). It is important to use the gifts He gave us with boldness. 1 Peter 4:10 tells us, "As each one has received a gift, minister it to one another, as good stewards of the manifold grace of God". I look to the example of David, one of the most talented worship leaders in history.

2 Samuel 6:14 says, "Then David danced before the Lord with all his might". All his might! That is a far cry from a subtle sway or an incognito step-touch.

I may never know what kind of harvest resulted from those trips to Greece and Mexico, but the glimpses I have seen tell me there was more beneath the surface. God showed me the tomatoes, but there were definitely some potatoes down there, too.

After my sophomore year, I spent the summer in New Jersey at South Mountain Community Church (SMCC) as a summer missionary, along with a team of eight other college students. We did a lot of servant evangelism; we handed out breakfast bars to commuters, we gave away free gasoline, and we passed out popcorn and snow cones at a 5k race. We helped the local church plant put on Vacation Bible School, run children's church, and lead worship.

Daniel and I built a strong relationship with the pastor and his family. We planned on returning to SMCC after graduation and our wedding, but God had other plans, and South Mountain Community Church closed its doors. We still keep up with this family, but with the church's closure, we are unable to see what became of the seeds we planted. And that's okay. I trust in God, and I believe He had us there for a reason. We quickly realized we would be used in the greater Baton Rouge area instead.

The song, *God of This City* was popular at this time, and I reflected on the chorus, which says, "For greater things have yet to come, and greater things are still to be done in this city[3]". God knew what our paths would look like, even when we did not.

Again, God planted seeds in my own life. After graduation I used the skills I learned in children's ministry at SMCC to get a job as a part-time children's minister at Oak Grove Baptist Church in Prairieville, Louisiana. Nearly eight years later, I can tell you, God knew I had a family waiting at this church. Almost every single time God's plans have looked different than mine, I've seen the beauty in His harvest eventually. I only say *almost* because some plans haven't come to fruition yet, but I fully believe they will. Not every flower blooms quickly. Evidently, the sheep-eating plant, or the Puya chilensis, takes up to fifteen years to bloom[4]!

I say all this to explain that God has unique timing. It is nothing like the timing we understand. We live in a world of instant gratification. We get upset when we don't get "likes" immediately after posting pictures on Instagram, or when our food takes too long to be delivered at restaurants. We want drive-thru service everywhere, and heaven forbid, something isn't available for two-day shipping on Amazon. We live in a world where we can send a message across the globe within seconds or learn about world news within minutes. Waiting is hard.

Plants do not grow overnight. We plant seeds, provide nutritious soil, water, sunlight, and then we wait. We forget God's affinity for gardening. Sometimes we need a little, well, a lot of cultivating. God knows the perfect soil for each of our needs. He knows when we need a little rain or a few days of sunshine. He knows when we need a good pep talk, much like George Washington Carver knew how to talk to his peanut plants.

When we grow impatient, let us remember the flowers. Go buy yourself a bouquet while you wait, or plant something pretty. God paid close attention to each hue, to each stripe, and to each leaf on the flowers. You know He cares even more for you. When God says wait, He means business. He's got a word for you, and it's in your best interest to listen. Let that garden grow!

3

Planting Desires

"Delight yourself also in the Lord, and He shall give you the desires of your heart." Psalm 37:4

God plants seeds within our hearts, which help us grow into the individuals He has cultivated. I believe God planted seeds in my heart that led me to the job I have today. I remember as a child, I had a friend with leukemia. I didn't know her well, but her picture remained on our refrigerator until she went into remission, and probably for some years after. She was the first person I ever knew with cancer, and I was genuinely concerned about what she was going through. A few years later, a classmate, whom I had never met, was going through treatment for leukemia as well. I volunteered to be his "buddy", and I made sure his folder was full of the things we had done throughout the week for his mom to pick up on Mondays. Stories of children battling cancer struck a chord in my heart each time I heard about them. I didn't even mind completing the Math-A-Thon workbook in fifth grade, because I knew it supported St. Jude Children's Research Hospital somehow. I remember sitting at a dance competition, watching my younger sister compete, and a small child with a beautiful, bald head walked by. It wasn't a significant event, but I still remember thinking "How can I help?" God was planting seeds in my heart.

Fast forward to college. I began my freshman year as an Apparel Design major. I figured I had a sewing machine, I enjoyed making my own designs, Project Runway was popular at the time, why not? But I remember feeling like I absolutely did not fit in with the other students in my classes. What I really wanted to do was create my own line of prom dresses to donate to teenagers with cancer. It would be called PROMises. I had a logo and everything, which I doodled while in business calculus. I hadn't put the connection together yet, that maybe God was shaping my heart for something else.

That same year, I went on my mission trip to Allende, Mexico. I had the humbling opportunity to work with children in less than ideal living conditions. Our team led vacation Bible school for a group of twenty to thirty children, and I was hooked. God was stirring my excitement for work with children. I came home changed and longing for a major I could put my heart into. I had already met with my advisor for the next semester and signed up for classes in Apparel Design, but I pulled out the course catalog and scanned the flow charts to put together a semester in Family and Child Studies. My heart was singing. At the time, I thought I would be a children's minister. From there, I volunteered with various churches, I babysat, and I worked at a school in the aftercare program there. I poured myself into working with children.

Toward the end of the next semester, I had to choose an internship site for my course work. I planned on using the school where I worked, since I already had a relationship with the families and staff. But my professor said something for which I will be forever grateful. He told us not to choose a site because it's comfortable. He encouraged us to read previous students' accounts of their internships and broaden our horizons. It was in that binder of essays where I learned about the child life profession. I read about a job where individuals work with children in hospitals to support normalization through play and preparation. It involved working in a hospital playroom, distracting children from their hospitalization and procedures, and keeping siblings involved and aware of the plans of care. I had only seen a glimpse of child life, but I knew I was onto something great. I immediately made plans to do my internship at the local children's hospital, and I never looked back. I went through the necessary steps during the rest of college and after to become a Certified Child Life Specialist, and now I work in our hematology/oncology unit with patients just like the children God used to spark my interest years ago. God was behind the scenes, in the garden, sowing seeds and tilling the soil in my heart.

He knew He was preparing me in New Jersey for a position in children's ministry, and He knew He was preparing my heart for a career in health care from an early age. He knew I would toy with the idea of becoming a pediatrician in the fifth grade, only to be scared by the thought of blood and death: two things I now see regularly. Had I gone down the path of a physician, I would not have the distinctive relationship I get to enjoy as a child life specialist. To be honest, I would have struggled through medical school, if I made it to that point at all.

I love all of Andrew Peterson's music, but I have to say one of my favorites of his songs is *Planting Trees*. One of the verses says, "So sit down and write that letter, sign up and join the fight, sink in to all that matters, step out into the light, let go of all that's passing, lift up the least of these, lean into something lasting, planting trees". If we fail to plant because we are fearful of the wait, we will never see a harvest. God will not let our work in His name go to waste. Galatians 6:9 tells us, "And let us not grow weary while doing good, for in due season we shall reap if we do not lose heart." Did you catch that last part? IF we do not lose heart.

We are in this life for the long haul, yet our lives are truly but a moment. Let's view our work in the scope of eternity and enjoy the harvest when it comes.

4

Parable of the Sower

Then He spoke many things to them in parables, saying: "Behold, a sower went out to sow. And as he sowed, some seed fell by the wayside; and the birds came and devoured them. Some fell on stony places, where they did not have much earth; and they immediately sprang up because they had no depth of earth. But when the sun was up they were scorched, and because they had no root they withered away. And some fell among thorns, and the thorns sprang up and choked them. But others fell on good ground and yielded a crop: some a hundredfold, some sixty, some thirty. He who has ears to hear, let him hear!" Matthew 13:3-9

Jesus spoke in parables. He was a storyteller. I learn by seeing examples or hearing stories, so these parables usually speak straight to my heart. The fact that Jesus chose a gardening analogy also further supports this idea of God as a Gardener. Let's look at this parable more closely.

Jesus is describing our relationships with Him. He walks

us through four scenarios in which the Word of God was spoken. Jesus explains what each scattered seed represents in verses 19-23: *"When anyone hears the word of the kingdom, and does not understand it, then the wicked one comes and snatches away what was sown in his heart. This is he who received seed by the wayside. But he who received the seed on stony places, this is he who hears the word and immediately receives it with joy; yet he has no root in himself, but endures only for a while. For when tribulation or persecution arises because of the word, immediately he stumbles. Now he who received seed among the thorns is he who hears the word, and the cares of this world and the deceitfulness of riches choke the word, and he becomes unfruitful. But he who received seed on the good ground is he who hears the word and understands it, who indeed bears fruit and produces: some a hundredfold, some sixty, some thirty."*

First and foremost, I want to acknowledge the seeds: they are not bad in and of themselves. The seeds are not the problem. In other words, the Word of God is not the issue. From the beginning, Scripture has been something we can hold onto as Truth. How we handle Scripture is where we go wrong.

Let's look at the first seeds. These seeds were sown, but scattered, and were ultimately eaten by birds. Jesus explained this represented people who hear but do not understand. These hearers may have been invited to listen to Jesus speak but had no follow-up. Their friends and coworkers may have disregarded His teaching as foolishness, and the hearers moved on with their lives without digging any deeper.

I associate this example with church campers. I know a lot of lifelong decisions are made at church camps. I spent my fair share of time at Girls in Action camps and youth camps growing up, and all of the experiences, in one way or another, left me with a better understanding of God. However, I am talking about the kids who are invited by friends, who are not from Christian homes, and whose acquaintances don't understand the importance of accountability yet. They are overwhelmed with emotional highs from the week and excited for the new life they committed to. Unfortunately, though, these decisions are hard to keep up with when there aren't any consistent teachers in their lives to cultivate the seeds that were planted. These are the seeds snatched up by birds.

Obviously, this can happen in any number of settings. I don't want to pick on church camps by any means! It could be a situation with an office worker who had a lunchtime spiritual conversation with a temporary employee, and didn't ever follow up. It could be a situation with a college student who received a tract about salvation. Or, it could be an instance of parents whose children went to Sunday School with limited understanding of the Bible stories, but they didn't make time for church themselves.

How do we reach out to those people?

I learned the meaning of the word "intentional" in the college ministry I was involved with. We learned that acts of service, such as paying for students' laundry, were not enough, in and of themselves, to lead others to Christ. We needed to further that conversation to truly show the campus who God was and is. I learned to be *intentional* when praying for people on prayer walks. I was *intentional* with the elementary school kids I watched in after school care. Every conversation had a purpose. I learned to make sure others understood who Jesus was, and what His death on the cross and resurrection meant. Did it go according to plan every time? No. Was I completely obedient in this intentionality? No. But it was a springboard for a new way of ministering to others.

The second group of seeds fell on shallow ground. These people know the basics. They may have attended Sunday School, and they may know John 3:16, but that is the depth of their relationship with Christ. This group of people may attend church on Sundays, but they don't pick up a Bible during the week. They like the term "fire insurance". Is their salvation any less legitimate than mine? Probably not, as long as they made a genuine commitment to the Lord. But let me put it this way: Say you married someone, promised to have and to hold as long as you both shall live, but you only spoke once a week for up to two hours. You didn't tell anyone about your spouse, and the only thing you confidently knew about him or her was a date and location of birth. Sometimes you checked in at meal times or on holidays. Great relationship, right? How easy would it be for your eyes to wander? How long would you last on "The Newlywed Game"? You see, when we have a shallow relationship with God, it's at risk of fizzling out, and not for His lack of trying, I can assure you. You can read in Revelation 3:16, "So then, because you are lukewarm, and neither cold nor hot, I will vomit you out of My mouth." Vomit is a pretty strong word with a lot of imagery and smells attached. Vomit is ultimate rejection. These seeds have no roots, and ultimately have nothing to hold onto when trouble comes. This relationship cannot live; these seeds cannot live, just like those eaten by the birds.

Next we come to the seeds among thorns. These seeds were given the Word. They understood, they may have learned a few Bible verses, but when the going got rough, they went running. In a matter of fight or flight, they flee. I have seen many people turn from God when they experience death of a loved one or a physical injury. They feel that God has taken something from them, and they aren't willing to walk with Him through the trial. They balk at the proverbial thorn in their sides.

The Bible is <u>very</u> clear about trials. James 1:2-3 says, "My brethren, count it all joy when you fall into various trials, knowing that the testing of your faith produces patience." When, not if. Life traumas will most definitely test a person's faith. It is normal to question the circumstances, but instead of questioning God's motives, question how He will use this for His glory and your good. We know the truth in Jeremiah 29:11, "For I know the thoughts that I think toward you, says the Lord, thoughts of peace and not of evil, to give you a future and a hope." Nothing in our lives is meant for harm. This does not mean we will not experience hardship, but it does mean God will not let a tear be wasted. Each and every sad or trying circumstance will be used to further His kingdom. Don't let your seed get choked by thorns. You get some weed killer and get after it!

Finally, we reach the good soil. I am ready for some good news after all of that! So these seeds are scattered in fertile soil, rich for the harvest, and ready to produce abundantly. These seeds are planted and cultivated, and their resulting crops are shared with others. These seeds represent people who hear the Gospel and run with it, not from it. These people seek after God and live up to the name Christian as it was intended: Christ follower. These people study God's Word and hang on every line. They hide His Word in their hearts (see Psalm 119:11). They share the Gospel with others, and they live a life that points to God and eternity. This is what we are aiming for. "He who has ears to hear let him hear!" (Mark 4:9)

Create good soil in your life. Spend time in prayer, even when you aren't about to eat a meal. Set time apart to sit in the stillness as you talk to God. Remember, conversations are two ways. Be quiet once in a while and let the Holy Spirit move in your life. Memorize scripture. Read books of the Bible, other than Psalms and Proverbs. I promise, there's some good stuff in there! If you have a hard time, use a Bible app on your phone that will give you a reading plan or daily devotionals. There is even a function to set a reminder on your phone. Read your Bible with a highlighter and pen in hand. I understand some people are uncomfortable writing in their Bibles, and that's okay! Get a journal and take notes. Really study it. You wouldn't just read a few chapters of a book for school (I hope!) We shouldn't treat the Bible that way either.

I hope you can read the Parable of the Sower with fresh eyes. Our Divine Gardener taught us a lesson with one of His favorite topics. I think that is a good enough reason to listen. Pray for those "seeds" who need good soil. Live a life of intention, one where you can share your knowledge of and experience with Christ. If you feel the Holy Spirit moving, follow! The more time you spend with God, the more aware of His presence you'll be. Our Gardener is always at work; we just have to look.

5

You Reap What You Sow

"But this I say: He who sows sparingly will also reap sparingly, and he who sows bountifully will also reap bountifully." -2 Corinthians 9:6

We've spent some good time talking about soil, but since the Bible mentions it in multiple contexts, I think we could benefit from another perspective. I want to focus on *what* we are sowing. When a farmer is ready to produce a crop, he first has to decide exactly which crop he wants to plant. He has to plan ahead, research when to plant it, how to tend to it, and figure out how long it might take to harvest. Notice: his production begins with a *decision* to grow.

The phrase, "you reap what you sow" is almost cliché because of its overuse. You get out of it what you put into it. You get what you give. Karma. There are many variations. But I want to focus on the biblical root. (Root? See what I did there?)

As we saw with the Parable of the Sower, sowing refers to planting God's Word in someone's heart. If we teach a lot of people about the gospel, chances are some of them will come to Christ. If we only teach one person, or none at all, our chances decrease or dissipate. Here's the thing: we've all been called to share the Word of God. We all have a responsibility to teach the gospel. How we do that, though, might differ from our fellow believers.

When I share the gospel, it might look like a classroom full of first graders and me with a Bible lesson. When my friend shares the gospel, it looks like a prayer with a stranger at a gas station. We are teaching the same message and sharing the same amount of love with others, it just shows up in different capacities. One isn't any more special than the other because we are both obeying God's call for our lives.

My sweet friend expressed the other day that she was struggling with her call to preach. She has spent years being the stronger Christian leader in her family. Her husband struggled with addiction, and she was left to raise her children in the church alone. God has miraculously delivered her husband from drugs, and he is now one of the boldest Christian men I know. He helps the homeless, he seeks out the lost, he listens to the Holy Spirit's beckoning calls to pray OUT LOUD with people he comes across each day. He is truly a walking miracle and a testament of God's healing power.

My friend said she felt unequally yoked because of how on fire her husband has become. But what she is forgetting is that for years, she was the soil nourishing her family. God planted her husband and her children in her life so she could, through Him, cultivate a body of believers. Her husband may look like a brilliant flower right now, but that beauty emerged after our Gardener used this faithful woman's calling to persevere.

My garden won't look like your garden. There will be days you feel like a flower, and others you feel like dirt or a seed. The beautiful thing about life is that God is still working in us. We can't ever say we have arrived, or that we did this thing on our own. A gardener's work is never done.

Flowers bloom and fade, and bloom and fade all over again. The old must be removed to make room for new growth, but the old can be reused for new soil to nourish baby seeds. We must not ever stop learning from our past.

It is work. Like I said before, we must choose to take care of our garden each day. We continue to pour into our seeds which have been entrusted to us. We continue to give them access to the sun (Son). We pull away the weeds that seek to destroy, and we ask God to provide the nutrients and climate we need for growth and sustainability.

Do not let your different tools hinder you from obeying God's command to spread the gospel. Regardless of how God has called you to do it, we all have a responsibility to tell others about Christ. Don't settle for a small harvest because you were jealous or scared or insecure. Reap a lot because you sowed a lot. You may need to be soil right now, but you may also need to benefit from the beauty of someone else's petals before you can become a flower yourself.

Not every flower is fragrant. Not every flower is used for tea or medicine. Not every flower deters mosquitoes. No two flowers are identical, even though God made them all. We can appreciate their intricacies and subtle differences. And they are so much like us. We may all be human, but we have different jobs to do. We can distinguish ourselves from one another, yet we all play a role in the Kingdom of God.

What *can* cause trouble is deciding not to sow, either out of feelings of inadequacy or frustration with circumstances. Say my friend became discouraged by her growth in comparison with her husband's, and she decided to stop teaching others about Christ altogether. Then her seemingly small harvest (according to her own evaluation) would become eradicated. That is when she would truly have a problem of disobedience. She prayed about her feelings and she brought her situation to a group of trusted women in Bible study. We were able to talk with her and point out ways she was faithfully sowing.

We continue to pray for her heart and her harvest that is her family. Sometimes we just need someone with an outside perspective to see our crops in a different light. And prayer. We always need prayer.

Don't get discouraged when your calling is different than someone else's. There is always a reason why God called us to a certain area of ministry. We must choose to sow each and every day. We may not see the harvest, or feel as useful as another person, but God assures us we will reap if we are faithful.

Flowers Don't Worry

*So why do you worry about clothing? Consider the lilies of the field, how they grow: they neither toil nor spin; and yet I say to you that even Solomon in all his glory was not arrayed like one of these. Now if God so clothes the grass of the field, which today is, and tomorrow is thrown into the oven, will He not much more clothe you, O you of little faith? –*Matthew 6:28-30

Here's the thing. I'm a worrier. I make up the most absurd scenarios in my head about what can go wrong. Part of my problem is working in a hospital. A doctor once told me there is this concept of "med school psychosis". Once you start learning about and seeing all these diagnoses and ailments, you start giving yourself symptoms, but in the words of Arnold Schwarzenegger, "It's not a tumor[5]".

Most of the things I worry about never come to fruition. I can lay awake and give myself a stomachache or work up a good sweat over nothing. God is <u>very</u> specific about worry. I quote Philippians 4:6-7 often: *"Be anxious for nothing, but in everything by prayer and supplication, with thanksgiving, let your requests be made known to God; and the peace of God, which surpasses all understanding, will guard your hearts and minds through Christ Jesus."* That, my friends, would be a command, not a suggestion. Do not worry. Just like "do not steal". So, that means it is a sin to worry. Take a minute to think about that one. I know I get a little defensive when I hear that, because I'm guilty a lot of the time. When we worry, we're saying we don't trust God enough to let Him handle it. And when was the last time our hair-brained scheme was better than what our Lord and Savior planned?

When I began to consider worrying as a sin, it really hit me in the gut. I cringe when I think of all the times I let worry get in the way of trust. Why is it so easy to slip into this mindset, when we know all things work together for our good (see Romans 8:28)? I'll tell you— because sometimes God asks us to do really hard things. Our outcomes are not always His outcomes. The answer to a prayer might be something sad, devastating even. We may not see the "why" behind it until later or even on the other side of eternity. But trusting God means we let Him have the reigns, no matter the outcome.

Like we saw in James, we *will* have trials, it is just a matter of when. Another example of this is in Psalm 23. This is a very popular Psalm, but I think it tends to become rote, and we lose sight of what David said. Check out verse 4:

> *Yea, though I walk through the valley of the*
> *shadow of death,*
> *I will fear no evil;*
> *For You are with me;*
> *Your rod and Your staff, they comfort me.*

This is definitive. David said He was walking through the valley of the shadow of death. It's not a "God, please don't send me to the scary places, let me bask in sunshine and daisies all the days of my life, amen" kind of prayer. It's bold. *I will fear no evil.*

Why could David fear no evil? Was it because he defeated Goliath as an underdog (1 Samuel 17)? Sure wasn't. Was it because he was a king? Nope. It was because He had God on his side. And we have God on our side, too.

So where do we start?

One thing that has been incredibly helpful for me is memorizing Scripture. I finished Beth Moore's study of the book of James several years ago, and one of the challenges was to memorize the entire book. I have always been pretty good at memorizing, so I figured, "Let's do this!" It's 108 verses. I thought about all the songs, phone numbers, birthdays, etc. I know by heart, and I decided it had to be doable. I added a verse a day, and spent my commute to work in the morning reciting passages. After a few months, I had it down. I printed out my certificate, I quoted the book to my husband, and then later at our annual women's retreat. While I don't practice it every day anymore, there are many chunks I still know very well. There are key verses I go to often.

I truly believe in "hiding God's Word in my heart" (see Psalm 119:11). God has given us His Word to learn more about Him, to help others, and to know how to live our lives, but if we only have it in a book, we aren't doing it justice. When I am discouraged at work, feeling like I'm not accomplishing my intended goals, I can immediately lean on Galatians 6:9, which says, "And let us not grow weary while doing good, for in due season we shall reap if we do not lose heart." When I am saddened by devastation, I can "taste and see that the Lord is good" (Psalm 34:8), no matter the circumstances. When I let my mind wander in the middle of the night, I can repeat, "When I'm afraid, I put my trust in You" (Psalm 56:3).

From a young age, my mom taught me to pray when I couldn't sleep. Psalm 56:3 is a verse I learned as a little girl. I had forgotten that child-like faith until a dear friend at church said quoting scripture was how she could easily fall back asleep in the middle of the night. Reading God's promises is a great way to settle my mind, but it is hard to get out of bed at 2AM to find a Bible. When they are in my memory, I have easy access and peace of mind. I know we do not have a finite amount of storage space in our brains, but it helps me to visualize the idea that the more Scripture I have in my mind, the less room there is for trash.

I know memorizing Scripture can seem like a daunting task, but let me tell you about my now five-year-old, Hudson. He struggled for a while with being scared of the dark and having bad dreams. I taught him Psalm 56:3, and I explained that he could recite it when he felt scared. We talked about a game plan for when he woke up in the middle of the night, and he decided on saying that verse over and over again until he could fall asleep. Eventually, he wanted a second verse to add to it. I taught him Proverbs 3:5, "Trust in the Lord with all your heart, and lean not on your own understanding". Flash forward a few months, and Hudson now knows about a dozen verses by heart. They vary in length, but he has a whole barrage of Scriptures to combat his fears. We usually pick a few each night to say before he goes to sleep, but some nights we roll through them all.

Not one to be left out, my three-year-old, Harrison, decided he wanted to learn a few verses too, so he chimes in with Psalm 34:8, "Taste and see that the Lord is good", and Psalm 118:24, "This is the day the Lord has made; we will rejoice and be glad in it". If my three-year-old can do it, so can you.

Another concept that has also helped with my worry is looking at things from an eternal perspective. The absolute worst thing that can happen is I die or someone I love dies.

I know—that is a terrible thing. One that makes me sick to my stomach to just think about. But as a Christian, I know death means I enter into eternal life with Jesus. So if the unimaginable happens, and my life or my loved one's life is taken, I can rest assured that God's promise of eternal life with Him stands strong. Should I die while my children are young, yes, that would be earth-shattering, but their lives would move on. They would learn to cope, and continue to function. (Although, I would hope they would need counseling at the very least. I'm super important, after all. I am kidding. Kind of.)

Looking at life through this perspective will definitely push you to stretch your trust in God. Learning not to worry is an exercise of faith. And like most exercise, it provides great benefits in the long run, but it is uncomfortable for a little while. Trust does not just happen. Think about earthly relationships. We build trust with others over time. Moms tend to struggle to find babysitters they trust with their children. Couples may look for a bank they trust before opening an account. We watch debates and read articles about which presidential candidate is the most trustworthy to run our country. Why would we think trusting God is any different? Let me clarify. God is faithful. He is not trying to prove His trustworthiness to us, but we have to build that trust from our end. We have to let go long enough to see God at work before we can get it into our minds that He will always do what is best. But we also have to remember to look at the big picture.

When it comes to trust, flowers can teach us a thing or two. Flowers have a lot of noteworthy characteristics. They are vibrant, colorful, exotic, and fragrant. They spend the day being taken care of by the bees, the sun, and the rain. They do not have a worry in the world. They know God will provide their needs, and like our verses in Matthew 6 tell us, if God can watch over the flowers, how much more will He watch over us?

It may seem counterintuitive, but if we want to stop worrying, we have to let go. One of my very favorite verses is Psalm 46:10, which says, "Be still and know that I am God". Our control issues tell us to fix things ourselves. We are reluctant to ask for help because our helpers may do things differently from us (i.e. wrong). But when we let God take the reins, we are giving them to the Expert, our Master, our all-knowing God. Fully trusting in Him is the only real key to eliminating worry from our practice.

The more we know Him, the more we can trust Him. We must stop trying to fix things and learn to turn them over to God. Be a flower.

7

Pruning and Weeding

Every branch in Me that does not bear fruit He takes away; and every branch that bears fruit He prunes, that it may bear more fruit. –John 15:2

I so wish I had a green thumb. I have tried and tried, and failed and failed, to keep plants alive. I have gone through countless hanging baskets on my front porch. I just love the color they add to my house. Until they die, and my house looks like the Addams Family's. A few years ago, my coworker bought everyone in our office these precious little bamboo trees for our desks. It was the cutest thing. I took pride in watering my plant every few days; I would hold it to my ear, and gently lift the stalk up and down to listen for excess water. I was meticulous in caring for it; I Googled ways to help it thrive, but it died on me anyway. (In all fairness, all but one died, so I feel like it's not entirely my fault.) Then I had the most beautiful hibiscus flower that lasted a few months. I just knew it was going to break the dying streak, but one cold snap, and it was done. My husband, Daniel, planted two lemon trees for me for Mother's Day last year, and the verdict is still out. It came with lemons, but we haven't seen any more since.

Daniel keeps up a fabulous vegetable garden, and I am both grateful and envious. It has always been his project, what with the plant killer streak and all, but I try to help as much as possible. One thing I have learned about is pruning. I learned how to prune as a child, when my mom would let me help with the houseplants. I knew to pull off the brown leaves, but I never understood it as more than a cosmetic task. It definitely wasn't one I minded; it was way easier than dusting.

Now that I'm older, I see why we prune. Out with the old, in with the new. When we pull away dead leaves, the plant knows to produce more fruit or flowers, depending on what kind of plant it is. Now who came up with that brilliant system? Oh wait, our Master Gardener!

Once again, God gave us a visual of what we need to do with our hearts. Sometimes we experience situations in life that prevent us from moving forward. Once we recognize them, it's time to bring out the shears. The difference between pruning and weeding is this: pruning is removing things that aren't inherently bad, and weeding is removing something toxic. Pruning can even be removing what is good for what is better. Think of fasting, for instance. We need food to live, but when we fast for a given time, we make room for God to grow. Spending time with friends can be really beneficial, but sometimes we need to skip a movie or a trip to the mall to have a quiet time with God. It's not the popular answer, but it is something we will be thankful for later. It may not mean cutting something out of your life completely, but setting it aside for a while.

I am about to go on a tangent for a second, but I promise, there really is a point. Another aspect of gardening I have learned about is composting. Some days I feel like a hippie, but I have grown to love our composting bin. And by "love", I mean it completely disgusts me, but I feel like I'm benefitting the earth by reusing our eggshells and apple cores. If you aren't familiar with a compost bin, let me give you a quick rundown. We have a jar next to our sink where we place pieces of produce that will not be eaten (peels, cores, leaves, or "lettuce" as my three-year-old calls any green parts), tea bags, unbleached coffee filters, eggshells, and a few other random biodegradable items. Once this jar is full, we take it out to the compost bin in our back yard. It is a large, black drum, which is mounted on a stand. We dump the jar in, close and lock the door (don't forget to lock the door—trust me), and then rotate it to mix it up. There is a general rule that you add a ratio of one-part dry to one-part wet, so if we have a jar full of wet items, we add a bucket full of dry grass clippings to balance it out. This helps to keeps the smell at bay. Once this drum is full and it sits for a while, it will start to look like soil. This is added to the garden, and we start the growth process all over again.

So what does that long compost rant have to do with pruning? Here it is: The pieces you prune can be placed in the compost bin to break down and be used for something else later. Remember, the things we prune aren't bad, just unnecessary for growth. We do not place weeds in the compost because they will just infest your garden with more weeds when you spread the compost. The weeds don't break down like other greens. Weeds have to be completely eliminated, but we will get to that in a minute. The pruned items can still help with growth, but timing is key.

People pruning is a little different than plant pruning. Obviously, you can't reattach leaves once they have been pruned, but the underlying idea of infectiousness is still there. The dead leaves won't necessarily kill a plant, but they hinder growth. Weeds aim to destroy.

Spending time with our close friends (our "people") is so beneficial for growth, as people and as Christians, but only if we are spending time with friends who help us further our walk with Christ. We need people for accountability, teaching, and when we need to know if our kindergartener is acting normally or not. But we must not let these people take the place of God. We still need to go to God in prayer when we face a dilemma. We must recognize when we are placing our friends above God and then prune when necessary. Cut back, don't cut off.

Other things that may need pruning are hobbies. I will be the first to tell you, I love reading. I am at the tail end of a book challenge that gave a list of forty types of books to read within a year. They ranged from a political memoir to a murder mystery, to a bestselling young adult novel. I have really enjoyed reading genres I don't normally read, and I ended up reading over ninety books within the year, rather than the required forty. But within those ninety books have been words I try to avoid, immoral story lines, and some plots that were truly a waste of time. I spent hours reading for fun when I could have been spending time in prayer or reading the Bible. Just like spending time with friends, reading can be incredibly beneficial, even leisure reading, but in the future, I will be more mindful of the books I read and how much time I spend with my nose in them. Again, I need to cut back, not cut off.

If you're unsure, pray about it. Ask God to show you what needs to be pruned. When you are asking God to improve your relationship with Him, He absolutely will not turn you down. It may be difficult, like so many other aspects of walking with God, but it is necessary for growth. In the end, it places you closer to our Creator, and there is no better place I would rather be.

Weeding

> *For every tree is known by its own fruit. For men do not gather figs from thorns, nor do they gather grapes from a bramble bush-* Luke 6:44

Weeds are vicious. Like I said, I don't usually partake a lot in gardening, because I'm pretty terrible at it, but I did learn to weed this year. While it was hard work, I felt like I did a good job. Daniel and I recently spent a Saturday getting our garden ready for a new season. The garden had become overgrown with weeds. It looked terrible. He had to work on chopping up a tree limb that had fallen, and I attacked the weeds.

Shovel in hand, burn pile ready, garden gloves on, I got after it. I dug, I chopped, I scooped, I pulled, (I complained), I loaded, and I burned. Weeding is hard work! Just when I thought I was done, I would see another speck of green. The boys were digging in the dirt, and every now and then I caught them burying a runaway root. I took my job seriously, and within a few hours, we had a beautiful box of dirt. I understood the importance of getting those suckers out. Even one can be devastating to a harvest.

I have heard people describe "weeding out the bad" in life. People who struggle with addiction often need to leave behind old friends who fed their former habits. Staying in close proximity to those who shared that lifestyle, who do not understand the change, will pull you down. They must be cut out completely for change and growth to occur. Once again, weeds cannot get recycled in the compost bin. They must be destroyed.

Weeding is a lot harder than pruning; I didn't mind pruning. It required minimal effort. The amount of dirt I saw rinsing down my shower drain that day is enough to tell you, weeding is a tough business. My muscles ached, I was sweaty, I smelled awful, I had blisters on my hands, and I was worn out. The term "hot mess" comes to mind. But it was worth it. Out with the bad, in with the good. We now have a blank slate to start with, a big box of dirt in need of some compost, seeds, water, and love. We will enjoy a season of growth, and we will reap the benefits. We certainly understand that none of it will be possible without God.

Here lies the tricky thing about weeds though: they disguise themselves as flowers and plants. They are green, some are nice to look at, and they grow really fast. Before we know it, weeds may choke out a healthy plant. Metaphorical weeds in our lives may mimic the good. They may say the right words and do just enough to look and smell like a flower, but their motives are far from honorable. Remember, unlike pieces that need to be pruned, weeds do not just inhibit growth, they kill. They are dangerous to plants, and dangerous to us.

People can be deceptive when their needs are at stake. Misery loves company, right? If something feels wrong, it probably is. Go to God, seek out an elder in your church, and go to the people who hold you accountable. Pray for discernment over the situation, and grab the weed killer when you need it. Run— don't walk—away.

God ever so gently urges us to prune and weed. When we are in the Word and in tune with the Holy Spirit, His nudging is evident. Sometimes we need to say no to a project and prune a little. Sometimes we need to completely remove something from our lives through a weeding process. He will help us figure out the details. Unlike water and sunshine, pruning and weeding do not need to happen every day. A good gardener will recognize when it's time for those undertakings. If we treat our Bible like water and sunshine, our Master Gardener will let us know when to prune and weed.

Soon enough, you will have a beautiful garden that reflects the work of our Savior. You will see why pieces needed to be pulled, and the abundance that takes their place will bless you richly. When we follow His plan, we reap the benefits. Will our garden grow without hiccups? Surely not. It's not all roses, right? And even roses come with thorns. But we are God's masterpiece, thorns and all (see Ephesians 2:10).

8

Gethsemane

Then Jesus came with them to a place called Gethsemane, and said to the disciples, "Sit here while I go and pray over there." And He took with Him Peter and the two sons of Zebedee, and He began to be sorrowful and deeply distressed. Then He said to them, "My soul is exceedingly sorrowful, even to death. Stay here and watch with Me. - Matthew 26:36-38

When I'm in distress, I want to be as comfortable as possible. I need a nap in my bed or a good cry on my couch with pillows and a blanket. When Jesus was facing the unimaginable, a looming death on the cross, He went to a garden. His affinity for gardens is possibly the most evident here.

I picture Gethsemane full of trees. I imagine their canopies provided a cool shade from the hot sun. The trunks may have offered a resting place for Jesus to sit and pray or kneel in God's presence. The garden was full of foliage created by God. Jesus felt comfortable in these surroundings at a time when He needed peace. He needed to be in His sacred space, enveloped in His Father's handiwork.

I wonder if Jesus visited the garden any other times. Did He share a snack with the disciples in this garden? Did they take a nap in the awning of the trees? Did Jesus go there to pray often? I can't help but think it was a favorite site. It seems like it was familiar.

I think it's important to have a place of solace where we can go to pray and study the Bible. Many people choose to utilize a prayer closet or prayer room. I adjust my schedule to do my quiet time before my family wakes up, when I can sit on the couch in silence—just me, my Bible, journal, and pen. I have everything in my side table basket, ready to go. I enjoy the routine, and it has become "my spot". I lay aside my phone and I can focus on what I'm reading that day. I like to highlight important passages, study the cross-references, and journal my prayers. The chapters are not always "feel good" chunks of the Bible, but there is always something to learn. I have written out many prayers as I have dealt with worries or struggles. Yes, it's therapeutic, in that it makes me feel better, but it goes deeper than a feeling. Every day I spend time with God, I grow closer to Him. I am not who I was five years ago, last year, or even a week ago, praise the Lord! My quiet time has evolved along with my relationship with God.

When Jesus went to Gethsemane, it wasn't the first time He prayed with fervor. It may very well have been the most intense prayer session of His life, but it was built upon a solid foundation. Luke 22:44 says, "And being in agony, He prayed more earnestly. Then His sweat became like great drops of blood falling down to the ground". I don't know about you, but I have not, nor have I ever seen anyone sweat blood. I cannot imagine the power in this prayer. You cannot have this kind of conversation with just an acquaintance. This intensity stemmed from depth and familiarity

Jesus had a connection to God like no other, being His son, but also being fully God (see John 1:1). No one has, nor will they ever, understand God like Jesus did, but we can look at their relationship as something to aspire to. It doesn't matter where, but we need to have a sacred space that invites intimacy with God.

I see Jesus in the garden as a way of showing He was scared and He needed God to cultivate, nourish, and prepare Him for what was ahead. Jesus submitted to God as a seed to the Master Gardener when He said "nevertheless not My will, but Yours, be done" in Luke 22:42. He let God take the reins and do the hardest thing imaginable. Jesus understood the importance of the cross. He knew God's ultimate plan of salvation was in the works, and He was prepared to make the crucial sacrifice so we could experience eternal life with God.

We need to think of ourselves as seeds. Without a gardener, seeds are useless. Like the seeds in the Parable of the Sower, seeds can end up in situations that prevent growth. It takes the careful work of a sower to make sure seeds end up in fertile soil with adequate nourishment. In our case, this nourishment comes from time with God. The Bible is sunlight and prayer is our hydration from the Living Water Himself. In the story of the woman at the well, Jesus told the Samaritan woman, "But the water that I shall give him will become in him a fountain of water springing up into everlasting life" (John 4:14). This water is far more than we get from a little green watering can.

Placing ourselves "in the garden" puts us in a position of submission. We recognize we are not in control of our lives; We put ourselves at the liberty of our Master Gardener. James 4:7 says to "submit to God. Resist the devil and he will flee from you". What a promise! Plants' biggest threats are predators. Plants face destruction by birds, bugs, chemicals, humans, and weather. It is up to the gardener to appropriately plan for these hazards. They utilize all sorts of tactics like scarecrows, yard owls, strategic planting, pesticides, natural insecticides, etc. Our protection from harm comes from submitting ourselves to God, as the plants must submit to the gardener.

Just like with worry, it may sound a little counterintuitive to protect yourself by letting someone else handle it; but if anyone can handle our lives, it's the Maker Himself. He created us, and He has the bigger picture in mind when we cannot see beyond our struggles. Flowers do not worry, and neither do seeds. Jesus was not worried in the garden; He was distressed. I think they are two similar, but different, emotions. Jesus knew God would choose the right path, but He knew it would not be an easy road.

Have you ever seen an elapsed video of a seed growing? It looks like a painful process, if seeds could feel. The sprout bursts out of the shell of the seed as the stem becomes stable and leaves develop. Roots take longer to dig in, meaning the plant is vulnerable while it waits for stability. It's kind of disturbing to watch.

Wouldn't it be painful to review our growing process, though? I don't want to revisit who I used to be. I don't want to see those painful lessons I had to experience to finally understand. I am sure it would open up an old wound or two. However, look where that painful process can bring us. We become more mature Christians. We deepen our faith and broaden our trust. The seed that underwent a metamorphosis became nourishment or something of beauty as its roots grew deep in the earth, anchoring it down and strengthening the plant little by little.

In our moments of pain, we learn to rely heavily on our loving God. Our hearts soften and we become more aware of God's character. We learn what it means to truly rely on Him and feel "the peace of God, which surpasses all understanding", which "will guard your hearts and minds through Christ Jesus" (Philippians 4:7).

Jesus left Gethsemane with a deeper understanding of God. He left with an acceptance of God's plan for Him on the cross. He was so accepting, in fact, He responded to Simon Peter's cutting off the Roman soldier's ear by insisting, "Put your sword into the sheath. Shall I not drink the cup which My Father has given Me?" (John 18:11). Jesus willingly died on the cross because it's what God asked of Him. Jesus felt so strongly about God's plan that He not only accepted it, He defended it, and helped the very person who would lead Him to death.

Gethsemane represents a physical and emotional place Jesus needed to go to. He had to go to His physical place of peace to allow his mind to wrap around what He knew in His heart. The garden would have meant nothing without Jesus' figurative roots in God. The prayer that took place in Gethsemane was the result of a lifetime walking next to God, not just a few hours alone in a garden. There is nothing magical about praying in a certain spot, but environments can affect the way we pray. If we are worried about someone interrupting, we might be guarded and avoid depth. If we are distracted, we may never reach a point beyond the surface. There is a reason Jesus asked His disciples to keep watch. He needed to guarantee He would be alone because His prayer was of utmost importance.

Prayer is serious. It is more than repetitive poems or trite phrases. Prayer is where we meet with our Creator. It is our garden- where the growth happens. We must look to Jesus as an example for how we need to live our lives— why wouldn't we take His example of where to pray?

I'll leave you with the hymn, *In the Garden*. I love the beauty of nature described, but also the closeness of the relationship with God. Find your garden—don't wait! It will only help your prayer life.

I come to the garden alone,
While the dew is still on the roses,
And the voice I hear falling on my ear
The Son of God discloses.
And He walks with me, and He talks with me,
And He tells me I am His own;

And the joy we share as we tarry there,
None other has ever known.
He speaks, and the sound of His voice
Is so sweet the birds hush their singing,
And the melody that He gave to me
Within my heart is ringing.
I'd stay in the garden with Him,
Though the night around me be falling,
But He bids me go; through the voice of woe
His voice to me is calling[6].

9

When You're Waiting on a Camellia, but God Planted a Magnolia

Trust in the Lord with all your heart, and lean not on your own understanding; in all your ways acknowledge Him, and He shall direct your paths. -Proverbs 3:5-6 NKJV

There have been a lot of times in my life when I have pursued something God placed on my heart, only to find out He was leading me somewhere else. Sometimes I have been able to see how the long, scenic route has been just as important as the final destination. I am eagerly waiting to find out the purpose of other journeys, but I feel confident I may not fully realize why until I get to heaven. And that is okay. Sometimes you plant a seed, eagerly anticipating a camellia, and a magnolia blooms instead.

In Matthew 28, verses 19-20, Jesus left the earth with this statement: "Go therefore and make disciples of all the nations, baptizing them in the name of the Father and of the Son and of the Holy Spirit, teaching them to observe all things that I have commanded you; and lo, I am with you always, even to the end of the age." Jesus didn't tell His disciples exactly where to go. He didn't leave them a map, or list several cities that might need help. He just said "go". I think God has us go, sometimes to put us in a specific destination, sometimes to learn along the way, and sometimes to show our obedience. But just as He promised, He is always with us in our travels.

During my junior year of college, when Daniel and I were engaged, we made plans to move to New Jersey to work with South Mountain Community Church, where we had served as summer missionaries. We flew out there to look for apartments, check out potential internship sites for me, and make sure there were decent sushi restaurants readily available. When you are twenty-one, there are certain priorities. We had discussed learning how to acclimate to new weather (AKA snow), who would come stay with us on trips to New York City, and how asking for gift cards over gifts for our wedding would be more logical than more boxes to move. We were on top of it.

We hit a lot of roadblocks, but we still felt we needed to pursue this. Because Daniel was jumping into a ministry position straight out of college, he did not have a Master's degree in worship or ministry, nor the funds to earn one. The church plant was content with this, as long as Daniel's pastor would provide a letter saying he was ordained. Daniel and his pastor had differing views on a call to ministry, and after much theological discussion, his pastor did not write the letter. While we respected and supported his decision, it was a tough blow. Another problem was that the cost of living was quite different in New Jersey than Louisiana, so we would need part time jobs to make ends meet and probably require some support from family. It was definitely not ideal, but we continued to feel God leading us in this direction, and we knew He would provide our needs.

But then a door slammed shut.

The church plant did not have the funds to hire him anymore. And just a few months later, the church plant closed altogether. It sent our dreams into a tailspin. We had to quickly make new arrangements, as graduation, my child life internship deadline, and our wedding were approaching quickly.

As we wondered what we would do, we faithfully tilled our soil. We continued to pray and trust God. And we began to see our magnolia blooming. Not long after this, Daniel was hired to work at the job he still holds in Baton Rouge, and I was asked to apply for a job as a children's minister in a nearby church, which led us to our current home church where we still attend with friends who have become family. I accepted an internship in Baton Rouge, which led to the job I still have, and we still have the chance to lead worship each week. The same type of jobs we were moving to New Jersey for sprang up right in our own backyard. I still don't know if God was preparing our hearts for our ministries here in Louisiana or if He was asking us to show our obedience in following Him. Probably both. Either way, I'm grateful for the garden that bloomed. It wasn't a camellia, but it was equally beautiful. God's glory was still present, and our labor was not in vain.

More recently, Daniel was asked to apply for a job as a worship pastor in Alabama. We are even more settled now than we were eight years ago, so I was definitely not as ready to pick up and move as I had been at twenty-one. After much debate, a lot of prayer, and a couple visits to this new church, my heart softened, and I knew it was something we needed to seriously pursue. Doors seemed to open, and the proverbial stars were aligning. Daniel met with the pastor, a very good friend of ours, and he told them we were coming. Again, we looked at houses, I applied for jobs, and we felt things were falling into place... until I didn't get the job I had my heart set on. The job that became available the day Daniel was presented with the job opening. The job I thought was a perfect fit.

And then things really came tumbling down.

This time, nothing changed with the church, but *our* circumstances changed. We realized, financially, we were not in a place to move. We had a lot of things we needed to get in order before we could consider moving without a full time job for me, a slight pay cut for Daniel, and fewer health benefits for our family. It was not a situation of "don't let finances keep you from following God's calling on your life". It was a situation of financial responsibility that God had convicted us of failing to exhibit. So once again, our garden of magnolias bloomed, and we kissed the camellias goodbye. This time, we could see how God used this long, curvy, rocky road to point out a lack of financial maturity, and bring us to a place of serving Him with our money.

It was a confusing situation, but I was also reminded of Abraham in Genesis 22, when God tested His obedience by asking Abraham to sacrifice his only son, Isaac, the son on whom he had waited for a LONG time. Abraham brought his son to a mountain to make the sacrifice, with full trust in God, and God provided a ram in Isaac's place. (As a mother, I cannot even fathom the emotional torment of this task. I can only assume his wife, Sarah, either had no clue what was happening, or her reaction was not fit for Sunday School.) I know God asks us to prove our dedication to Him; This story is very clear. I am eternally grateful God has not asked us to give up something of this magnitude, but we have made small sacrifices along the way. I have been blessed through the trials, and I have learned valuable lessons along the way. Would I have rather gotten a handout on obedience? You betcha. But would that have sunk in? I can only assume not. God knows me better than I know myself.

In the end, we didn't pack up our house. We didn't resign

from our jobs. We remained in our home God provided, and we continued to lead worship on a volunteer basis with our little church family. I really struggled to accept it. I had begun to pull away from everyone and everything in Louisiana. My plans focused on Alabama, and nothing else. I didn't even really know what to do with my Kindergartener in August! I had neglected to pay close attention in the registration day— I went "just in case". I had counted my chickens before they hatched.

I still feel confident we heard Him clearly; I do not feel like Jonah avoiding Nineveh. I truly believe we did what we were supposed to do. If it was only to discover the financial trouble we were in, then I'm okay with that. I believe we still have work to do here in the Baton Rouge area, though.

In August of last year, 2016, Louisiana was met with the worst flooding we have seen in decades. As of right now, I've heard around 188,000 homes were affected[7]. Over 188,000 families lost homes, vehicles, family members, pets, and countless sentimental items. If we had been in Alabama, we would have only been gone two weeks, with no time off to speak of in new jobs, and no ability to help our brothers and sisters in need. Our pastor stopped Daniel and said, "I don't know why you chose to stay, but this is why you are here". I felt guilty because a small part of my mind had thought, "If we would have been gone, we wouldn't have had to deal with this devastation". But I don't really believe that. We would have driven ourselves crazy coming down on weekends or wondering if we made the right decision to leave. I know we are right where we need to be.

We did have to make a difficult call to our friends in Alabama, but they understood. Although I know we disappointed them, I also know they appreciated our honesty. This new friendship has forged the way for their church to send mission teams to help our church members who lost everything in the flood waters. Our relationship has continued to grow with our brothers and sisters in Christ, and it was quite unexpected, but more than welcomed. God knew that before it happened, too. We knew God planted a tree— what we thought was a camellia. We watered it, and we made sure it had sunlight. We waited patiently to see the flowers, and we imagined what the blossoms might look like. But then a magnolia sprang up- the beautiful state flower of Louisiana. It truly did not matter what God had planted; we were only asked to faithfully care for it. It was not what we were expecting, but it was beautiful growth, nonetheless.

Psalm 27:13 tells us, "I would have lost heart, unless I had believed that I would see the goodness of the Lord in the land of the living." I have not lost heart. I do not for one second believe God led us on a wild goose chase for His own entertainment. Although, I'm sure we were a sight to see. We will see His goodness through this ordeal. One day we will laugh about the 2016 craziness. Just as Paul wrote in Philippians 1:6, I am confident that "He who has begun a good work in you will complete it until the day of Jesus Christ".

Our Master Gardener plants all sorts of beautiful vegetables, trees, and flowers for us to take care of. Sometimes we have a cute little garden label telling us we are looking for tomatoes. Sometimes we can recognize the distinguishable leaves of aloe. He knows we sometimes need to be aware of what we are waiting for, but not always. Sometimes, really all the time, we need to trust Him with our produce. Whether we received a camellia or a magnolia, our job was clear: make time for God, above all, lead others in worship, make time for our family, and take care of our business.

We can, and will continue to see His goodness.

What if I'm the Magnolia?

Sometimes, we place our identity in a title, rather than in Christ. Sometimes we get wrapped up with being a camellia, when God wants us to be a magnolia. Both flowers are beautiful, and it is not a bad thing to be associated with either one. But if we become consumed with *what* we are over *Whose* we are, we run into problems.

When we faced the move to Alabama, I knew it meant that I would no longer be a child life specialist, for a little while, or perhaps forever. I struggled, because I worked hard for that title, and I felt like so much of my character revolved around my job. Through all of the Alabama journey, God taught me to let that go as well. I am a daughter of the King, and every action and position in life should filter down from this. It is not about my accomplishments or my skills. It is about what God has done.

Olympic diver, David Boudia, said it best, after winning a silver medal in Rio de Janeiro, Brazil. "There's been an enormous amount of pressure. I've felt it. It's just an identity crisis. When my mind is on this [diving], and I'm thinking I'm defined by this, then my mind goes crazy. But we both know that our identity is in Christ, and we're thankful for this opportunity to be able to dive in front of Brazil and in front of the United States. It's been an absolutely thrilling moment for us."[8]

If our earthly identities are found in being a parent, holding a job, our heritage, our skin color, our talents, or our possessions, we will be sorely disappointed. We must be aware of our need for God and be willing to identify ourselves through Him and Him alone.

A few weeks ago, my dad took a DNA test to find out where we came from. I thought it was pointless, since I knew we were Cherokee. My whole life, my grandmother has told me stories and taught me things about our heritage. I remember her taking me to a reservation and buying me a beautiful doll displaying traditional dress of the Cherokee. She has paintings and decorations in her house that reflect this culture. It is who we are.

So, as you might have guessed by now, his tests came back, and under Native American, was a big, fat ZERO percent. No Cherokee, whatsoever. In fact, we are Belgian. I have no clue where this disconnect came from. I protested, "This is a scam. We KNOW we are Cherokee. It has to be wrong." My step mom started explaining how it matched us with family members, and they sent pictures of people we were potentially related to, which had a scary resemblance to our family. My sister, Whitney, and I were given strict instructions not to tell my grandmother. (She has since been told, and had a good laugh.) Whitney, almost in tears, said "I don't even know who I am anymore!" I love her flair for the dramatic.

To be honest, not being Cherokee didn't really end up affecting my life in the least bit. I kind of enjoyed the funny story to tell. It was something we discussed in school while learning American history, but my daily life was not changed because of this revelation. Actually, being of Belgian descent explains my fair complexion a lot better than Native American does. I did not have an identity crisis over this. In heaven, it will not matter where I came from, only Who I am with.

Did I wake up one morning a camellia and go to bed a magnolia? Maybe, but I believe it really just means I'm the same flower, just bought from a different nursery. And I am okay with that. Again, I have learned that my identity has to come from Christ before anything else. Isaiah 40:8 says, "The grass withers, the flower fades, but the word of our God stands forever". That is where I want my identity to be. Something that lasts. My looks will not be the same forever. I'm pretty sure I have a new wrinkle on my forehead since yesterday. My job will not last forever. My possessions will not last forever. But God's Word? That is a solid rock. As long as I identify with Him, my circumstances can change a million times, and I will remain firm.

I can follow God on a crazy adventure only to end up in my backyard, and I still know His promises are true. He will never leave us, nor forsake us, whether that is in New Jersey, Alabama, Louisiana, or the next destination we feel led to go. I can be any flower, as long as I'm His flower. My Gardener has a plan, and I will lift my leaves to Him.

10

God Made Dirt, so Dirt Won't Hurt

When He had said these things, He spat on the ground and made clay with the saliva; and He anointed the eyes of the blind man with the clay. And He said to him, "Go, wash in the pool of Siloam" (which is translated, Sent). So he went and washed, and came back seeing. —John 9:6-7 NKJV

Life is messy. Rarely do we find ourselves in a cookie cutter plan, completed to fruition with no complications. We wake up on a normal Saturday, and end up in the emergency room with a spouse or child. We put on the cutest new top we bought on sale, only to spill coffee on it before work. We leave our house on time and get caught behind a wreck. A little dirt, a lot of dirt, it doesn't matter. It all makes a mess.

But are all the messes meaningless?

There have been mornings when I have tried my hardest to get out the door on time to arrive at work at or before 8AM. I set my alarm, I don't hit snooze, I don't try to fit in a bunch of extra chores, and I make my way through my morning routine. But then one of my sons has to use the bathroom, after he's fully dressed, or the dog gets out of the fence and runs across the neighborhood, or my work badge, which is *always* in my purse, is not there, it's in the parking lot at the grocery store (true story). Then in a huff, I fly out of the house, drop the boys off at school, and come upon an accident that probably happened at the exact time I would have been there, had I left on time. Those little messes can be our saving graces.

If God wanted life to always be clean, don't you think He would have made plants grow in something else? God created dirt; dirt sends us running to Him.

When we recognize we are filthy and we need a Savior, we stop depending on our own strengths and lean on our Creator. Plants have no choice but to lean on a gardener for support, but we tend to think we can do it all. The little messes of life can remind us in a split second of our inability to walk alone.

If we were all perfect, there would be no need for Jesus. God knew before we existed that we would have trouble. That we would make a mess of things. And still, He loves us. As Romans 5:8 tells us, "But God demonstrates His own love toward us, in that while we were still sinners, Christ died for us." God didn't wait for us to clean up before He told Jesus His mission. He chose to save us in all of our filth, looking like a bunch of Pig-Pens. He sees far beyond the mess.

Our sin makes us unclean. It is not a good look for us. But there is a "messy look" that is far more flattering. It is God's favorite, if I had to guess.

Some tasks of life require us to "get our hands dirty". Helping the poor can be an unclean job. Working in the medical field is messy. Helping victims of abuse is going to leave us with dirt under our fingernails; but all these are inherently good things. This is the kind of dirt we need. This dirt is the soil that nourishes our hearts and points us to the Savior, our Gardener. This good dirt can smell awful and get stuck on the bottoms of our shoes, but it's the dirt that helps us grow the most.

Jesus got dirty when He healed the blind man in John, chapter 9. He literally stuck his hands in the mud to give the man sight. He wasn't only touching someone untouchable, Jesus visibly soiled His hands. But it was so worth it to the blind man and to us, as we can benefit from learning of Jesus' healing power and compassion. This was good dirt.

Other biblical heroes such as Daniel, David, Paul, Stephen, and Esther all got dirty for the sake of the call. Look at the legacies they left behind! If they stayed in a clean little bubble of contentment their whole lives, we may not have the role models of how we should follow Christ which we still have to read about today. Or rather they would look much different. (God can and will work whether we choose to obey or not.)

Daniel ventured into a den of lions. Not only was he amidst some of the scariest, most powerful creatures on earth, facing death, he was in their waste. I am sure their enclosure was no fancy "habitat", but more of a dry mud hole. Once he realized they were not going to kill him, he might have had a chance to notice the smell. Ultimately, his desperation and discomfort led to dependence on God, which led to deliverance.

David most famously fought a messy, bloody battle against Goliath, ending in a beheading before a victory. He lived his young adulthood as a shepherd, in the fields, herding dirty animals. Blood, guts, and dirt. He also got himself into a metaphorical mess when he chose to take Bathsheba, another man's wife, as his own. He gave into temptation and let his eyes linger on her bathing body (see 2 Samuel 11). His mistake led to murder and the death of David and Bathsheba's child. The Bible is full of hot messes.

Paul, who began his career hating Christians, ended up writing most of the New Testament of the Bible, and represents one of the greatest missionaries of all time. He spent time in prison after preaching the Gospel. He walked on his fair share of dirt roads, and he made tents. All of which are outdoor jobs and would result in dusty feet and clothes after a long day of traveling or working. He was unafraid of dirt.

Our dear Stephen was the first known martyr. He was stoned to death as he laid on the dirty ground. He went out fighting the good fight for Jesus' ministry. I am sure as soon as he arrived in Heaven, Jesus wiped his dirt and tear streaked face with the most welcoming arms you ever did see.

And precious Esther. She stood up to King Xerxes and came for "a time such as this" (see Esther 4:14). I am certain she faced the king and rescued her people with sweat dripping down her temples and clammy hands. Not the fresh faced look she was going for, I would imagine. But she was full of good dirt, as with all the others.

If we are on our knees in prayer, we are bound to get dirty. God will call us out of our clean comfort zones and into a messy world. He will challenge us to dig in the dirt as we search for lost souls. We will most assuredly leave behind a muddy footprint for future generations to follow. We will develop some hard-to-reach dirt behind the ears, and it may take scrubbing, but we will be better for it.

It is okay to become filthy for the sake of being God's hands and feet. We want this kind of dirt. We need to experience the messiness to appreciate the cleanliness.

Still, there is a different kind of dirt. Sometimes we get dirty because we choose to wallow in the mud. In the parable of the Lost Son in Luke 15:11-32, the rebellious son takes off with his inheritance and essentially wastes it all. He gets

God's Green Earth

to the point of desperation where he willingly takes a job feeding and living among pigs. He chose the mud.

Just like the lost son, we are attracted to things of filth. We want to look like everyone else, when in reality, we need to spend our lives trying to look like our Savior. 1 Peter 1: 13-16 says "Therefore gird up the loins of your mind, be sober, and rest your hope fully upon the grace that is to be brought to you at the revelation of Jesus Christ; as obedient children, not conforming yourselves to the former lusts, *as* in your ignorance; but as He who called you is holy, you also be holy in all your conduct, because it is written, "Be holy, for I am holy". There isn't much room to wiggle there. This life of lust and ignorance covers us in the wrong kind of dirt. It makes us unappealing to God. Don't get me wrong, He loves us just the same, but we are not a pleasant-smelling, living sacrifice to Him when we cover ourselves in rubbish.

When we have houseguests or we plan to see someone important, we clean up. We bathe. We make sure we look our best and our home is in order. We get rid of, or at least, hide, the dirt. Filth is an embarrassment. We do not treat our earthly bodies this way when it comes to the dirt we have accumulated. It seems the thing to do is celebrate the grime, the rot, the uncleanliness. This is not how God intends us to live. According to 1 Peter 2:9, we are "a chosen generation, a royal priesthood, a holy nation, His own special people, that you may proclaim the praises of Him who called you out of darkness into His marvelous light".

See? He has delivered us from the dirt. He wants us to trade that life for light in Him. Do not confuse getting your hands dirty for wallowing in the mud. The thing about dirt is that in many cases it helps build character, perseverance, and courage, but we are not meant to live there forever. Like Isaiah 61:3 says, God will give us "beauty for ashes", "the planting of the Lord, that He may be glorified". Eventually, we make the trade. Eventually, the seed leaves the dirt to

57

grow into the flower. The colorful petals find themselves pointing to heaven, away from the dirt that brought them there. They leave the soil and point to the sun.

This is what we must do. Follow the example of the flowers, once again. Use the dirt to grow, but then leave the dirt, and point to the Son. The flowers we have helped along the way will be growing right beside us, and our Gardener will be more than pleased with our growth in Him. God made that dirt for a reason, and we will be smart to use it for His glory.

11

Vertical Gardening

*If then you were raised with Christ, seek those
things which are above, where Christ is, sitting
at the right hand of God. Set your mind on
things above, not on things on the earth. For
you died, and your life is hidden with Christ
in God.* –Colossians 3:3 (NKJV).

In Stephen Covey's best-selling book, *The Seven Habits
of Highly Effective People*, one principle is to "begin with
the end in mind"[9]. In other words, have a goal. What are
you working for? What are you striving for? Ultimately, we
should live our lives with eternal thinking.

As I have said before, I am by no means a real gardener,
but I do have a Pinterest account, and that makes up for a lot,
right? I think vertical gardening is fascinating and beautiful,
and something I am completely unsure of how to go about.
But I do love the concept as it relates to our relationship with
God on a vertical scale versus a horizontal one.

Vertical gardening seems to fall into two types: one
where the plants grow right up a wall and another where

the plants are potted and arranged along a wall. I think both are important in our comparison.

Some gardeners use vertical gardening to cover up an unsightly wall. I think we do a lot to cover up our insecurities and imperfections, but the best thing we can do is hide ourselves in Christ. I love Colossians 3:1-3, which says "If then you were raised with Christ, seek those things which are above, where Christ is, sitting at the right hand of God. Set your mind on things above, not on things on the earth. For you died, and your life is hidden with Christ in God." Look at how perfectly this fits too, with our talk of vertical relationships! We are looking above.

So what does this mean, to "hide ourselves in Christ"? Psalm 119:114 says, "You are my refuge and my shield; I have put my hope in Your Word." God can protect us from sin and shame if we let Him. When we hide ourselves in Christ, He becomes our safe place. He will protect us and hold us until we are, with His help and guidance, on our feet.

If you have ever played hide and seek, you know what it's like to be in a really good hiding spot. My husband is the hide and seek champion. The kids in our children's ministry play at church all the time— aren't churches the best for hide and seek? There's a great spot behind the old choir robes, there are closets galore, and very few things that can get broken. Daniel has been known to hide in the food warmer. (And he says he's a germophobe!) One time, as a child, he hid in the trunk of his mom's car in the church parking lot after an evening service. He knew no one would find him, because he brought the keys with him. His feeling of safety soon diminished after he realized no one *could* find him, it was dark, and dread washed over his preteen self. A few panicked parents and a call to Pop-A-Lock later, he was found.

See, Daniel's hiding place was flawed. Things could have gone extremely wrong, depending on what time of year it was in Louisiana. Thank God, the only baggage that came with the event is a funny story to tell. When we hide ourselves in Christ, we are not closing ourselves off to those around us. God made us to be relational, and going at it alone can be dangerous. Hiding in Christ means He becomes our filter. He helps us decide what comes in our minds and bodies and what goes out.

Much like the ugly wall hiding behind the vertical garden, when we hide in Christ, our old selves are put away. The walls we built are transformed into something beautiful, benefitting the world around them. An eyesore no longer, we are able to boldly proclaim the name of Christ and credit Him with our transformation. Hiding in Him gives us strength to speak up. Hiding in Him is not cowering or backing down, but standing firmly under His wings.

When space is an issue, vertical gardening in pots is ideal. For the neat and tidy people in my life, this section is for you. When a gardener dedicates a wall to a vertical garden, they may choose to make nice, neat sections for each plant. The wall is still being used in its entirety, but it has a different feel. I think it's easy for the visual learners to see God working in each aspect of life. One pot might be family, one home, one work, one friends, etc. We have many sections of ourselves, but ultimately, the pots make up one wall. God is over them all. Each pot is cultivated by the same gardener, with the same sun, and same irrigation system—because vertical gardens cannot just run on rain.

Arranging these pots takes some thought. The gardener has to map out the space and decide if the rows are to be evenly spaced or more organized chaos. He must decide if the pots will match or coordinate or show up helter-skelter, and he needs to choose which plants go in the pots. The gardener also needs to figure out how the plants will receive water and fertilizer.

I think this system is where I would start. Growing plants directly on the wall takes resources, time, energy, and dedication. The pots seem like a stepping stone to special fertilizing wall paper. I think this can be said for our lives in God. Giving God our pots is a perfect starting place. We start relinquishing each section of our lives until He has them all. We become so lost in His goodness and glory that we forget they were ours to begin with. We become so hidden in Him, to the point that the extra time and effort doesn't seem so daunting. Our vertical gardens point to heaven.

Now vertical thinking is something I struggle with. I remember trying to answer the question, "Why does God allow bad things to happen to good people?" as a teenager. I sat there, at a loss for words, because I really didn't know. I knew God was all powerful, and if He felt we needed to go through a hardship, then we did, but I couldn't get much farther than that. The truth is, no one is good, but God (see Mark 10:18). Bad things happen to people because sin entered the world. To say good people shouldn't experience bad things is to say the pretty flowers shouldn't get eaten by pests. We have to put aside the comparison game, and look at what God is doing in our lives instead. In other words, look up.

I will never forget learning this lesson from a fifteen-year-old boy, having just been diagnosed with lymphoma. His friends kept saying, "But you're the best guy we know! This isn't fair! Why would God let such a bad thing happen to such a good person?" His incredibly mature response was, "Who says I'm good? If it has to happen to someone, it might as well be me. It has nothing to do with how good or not good I am." I was in my early twenties at the time, but he definitely taught me a lot that day.

When our minds are perpetually looking to God, with eternity in mind, little annoyances and setbacks of life don't matter as much. We stop complaining and start thanking. We stop nit-picking and start loving. We stop worrying and start stepping out in faith. Satan hates it when we look up.

The longer we look down at our feet, the easier it is for him to sneak in. If our eyes are always on the ground, we will stumble.

When our eyes are up, it isn't a prideful thing. It is confidence in our Savior. We know nothing can destroy us because God is our refuge. Vertical gardens don't get trampled. They are nestled in their places on the wall. Sure, the same pests are still an issue, but their metaphorical eyes are up. They don't cower in fear because they don't know to do so. They are not comparing each other because they are too busy glorifying God.

Vertical thinking is constantly praising our Father, resulting in an outpouring of love for others and giving glory to God. Vertical gardens are a work of art, just like we are God's masterpiece (Ephesians 2:10). He created us to glorify Him, and looking to Him in all we do does just that. Psalm 121:1-2 says, "I lift up my eyes to the mountains- where does my help come from? My help comes from the Lord, the Maker of heaven and earth." (NIV). Our Master Gardener who made us, who made this world, deserves nothing but the best. Our entire selves should point to Him.

Maybe our first step is to cover the unsightly wall, our embarrassing past. Put away the old thinking and put on a new life in Christ. Just like Ephesians 4:23-24 says, "be renewed in the spirit of your mind, and that you put on the new man which was created according to God, in true righteousness and holiness." Let His love cover you so much that you realize how worthless a life of sin truly is.

Once you realize what it is to hide in Christ, start giving your pots to the Creator. Allow Him to work in your marriage, your job, your children, your hobbies, your finances. Slowly your pots become His. Your life becomes His. And you realize you don't want it any other way. As you give God your possessions and your most precious treasures, you will realize you are growing, and growing up. You are moving closer and closer to heaven and an eternity with the Master Gardener.

You will realize it is not just a trend or a phase. Your dependence on God will result in a richer walk. A deeper faith. A restored trust. Your inability to do life on your own will no longer be an insecurity, but a comfort. Paul described this paradox in 2 Corinthians 12:9, where he says, ""My grace is sufficient for you, for My strength is made perfect in weakness." Therefore, most gladly I will rather boast in my infirmities, that the power of Christ may rest upon me".

Look to Paul's example here. Place it all on the line, and give it to God. Hitting the wall may be the best thing to ever happen to you.

12

Cucumbers and Crocuses

One thing I have desired of the Lord, that will I seek: that I may dwell in the house of the Lord all the days of my life, to behold the beauty of the Lord, and to inquire in His temple. - Psalm 27:4

There is so much beauty in the Lord. His love for us is indescribable. His grace is more than we can ever earn or replicate. The way the Bible ties together is greater than any earthly story. Our God is beautiful, and He fills our world with beautiful things.

When I think about what we deserve, it can be disconcerting. If we got what we deserved, we would receive death and darkness. But God. God gave us His only Son, Jesus, to die on the cross, taking our place, and forgiving us of all our sin, allowing us to live with Him for all eternity (see John 3:16). His sacrifice is beautiful and oh so necessary.

Just like earthly gifts, there are those that are pleasurable and those that are beneficial. I like practical gifts, to an extent, but I really appreciate the gifts that are nice items I wouldn't buy for myself. They don't have to be costly, just a little something extra (We call that "lagniappe" in Louisiana). Think of it like this: I enjoy eating broccoli, asparagus, bell peppers, and cucumbers at meal times, but for my anniversary, I would definitely rather have a bouquet of sunflowers or gerbera daisies. On the other hand, if I sat down to eat with nothing but a beautiful centerpiece and an empty plate, I would be a cranky, hungry girl. God knows what we need, when we need it. And He knows we need spiritual vegetables and flowers.

The beauty in His gift is that it is both beautiful and beneficial. The relationship with God we strive for today would mean nothing without the Cross. His new covenant with us, or our ability to be forgiven for our sins and live for eternity with Him in heaven, is truly a gift. His love and mercy sustains us and allows us to see the loveliness in life.

Our Master Gardener seeks to sustain us. When I am weak, He provides encouragement through people, creation, and His Word. 2 Corinthians 4:16 says, "Therefore we do not lose heart. Even though our outward man is perishing, yet the inward man is being renewed day by day". God renews us by allowing us to rest in His presence, both spiritually and physically. I cannot tell you how many times I have fallen asleep, my mind in a dither, just coming to Him in prayer and reciting all the verses I can think of. He sets my body at rest so my mind can refresh the next day. It is never as bad after a good night's sleep. He also renews us by placing people in our lives to pray for us, say the right thing at the right time, or just love on us. A nice, seemingly random text of encouragement can boost my mood in seconds. I believe God places those urges within our hearts, knowing the recipient needs to hear a specific message in that moment. We need these "veggies"!

Eating vegetables keeps our immune system up; it helps

us stay strong, and keep our bodies functioning properly. God's gifts are beneficial to us in that they keep our spiritual immune systems functional. When we fall, we are able to get back up much more quickly if we are in a relationship with God. If we are regularly eating from the vegetables He gives us, we are able to know with confidence the Truth He has taught us. We are more aware of the devil's schemes and lies. We are less likely to stay in a cycle of sin. If our spiritual diet consists of junk, we will not withstand the heartaches of this life. Don't get me wrong, without God, we can't withstand them no matter what, even if we are chomping on spiritual kale at every chance we get.

God prepares us for trials, though, in our everyday interactions with Him. Like running a race or studying for a math test, you prepare ahead of time so the end result will be victorious. You practice similar distances or equations to become familiar with how to train your body or solve the problems. Studying the Bible does not physically prepare us for hardships, but we are able to look at real people who experienced unimaginable trials and see how God brought them through. We read about Hannah, who experienced struggles of infertility, Ruth, who lost her husband, Job, who lost everything, including his children, his wife, and his health, Moses who killed a man, Paul, who was imprisoned for his faith. The list goes on and on and on. These brothers and sisters in Christ are examples of God's provision, love, and mercy in our suffering and sorrow.

God most assuredly gives us what we need, but He also knows we thrive on beauty. He has created breathtaking landscapes for us to enjoy. He paints pictures in the sky to make commutes a little easier. He designed gorgeous flowers to look at and breathe in. Sometimes a rough drive to work is pacified by a flowerbed full of sunflowers on my walk to the office. A difficult week is remedied by a bouquet of bright blooms.

The Master Gardener renews us with visual reminders of His promises and power. After the floods in South Louisiana in 2016, residents saw rainbows over the flooded neighborhoods. While we were suffering loss and devastation, the rainbows reminded us of God's promise never to flood the whole earth again. Our hearts were restored because we knew, even in the darkness, His light would prevail.

When someone is sick in the hospital or at home, a bouquet of flowers can make the biggest difference. It adds color to an otherwise drab room, or changes the appearance of the same four walls, and the fragrance covers the often unpleasant smells of being ill. God designed those! Every petal, every seed, every leaf, every stem was created with purpose. We crave beauty because our Creator designed us to.

Flowers know this. They cannot contain their beauty. They do not hide their petals; they lift their heads in admiration to their Creator. Jeremiah 20:9 tells us that Jeremiah could not keep the Lord to himself. Flowers are the same way. They are in constant display of glory.

Flowers have a way of making other people admire the giver, too. Girls swoon over a presentation of roses, making the object of her affection that much more attractive. But who made those roses? Of course, God did. When we stop to thank God for His handiwork, we are living a life of worship. When we say a prayer of admiration for the sound of birds singing or for the palette of reds, oranges, yellows, and browns in the fall, we are worshiping God for His design.

Most of the time, we recognize God's beauty in flowers right away. When we consume vegetables, we typically recognize their value much later. Learning to look for God's beauty in nature helps us cultivate a grateful heart. It helps us understand God's character a little bit better in cooperation with spending time with God in prayer and the Bible.

We also learn that worship is not just singing a few

songs on a Sunday morning. It is so much more than that. Worship, by definition, is "reverent honor and homage paid to God or a sacred personage, or to any object regarded as sacred[10]." Notice, this definition does not mention anything about singing. When we honor God, we respect Him, love Him, show affection to Him, and share Him with others. Recognizing the beauty of creation as you walk or drive with a friend is an easy way to express your devotion to God. "Wow! God really outdid Himself on those wildflowers!" "God is so powerful— look at the way the lightning just dances across the sky!" Nature opens the door to insert God in conversation, and it could lead to more in depth "peas and carrots" topics.

Beholding a bouquet or admiring a sunset does not automatically prepare us for spiritual battle, but it can provide comfort when we are in the thick of it. God understands we need strength and rest, courage and comfort. When we "eat our vegetables", i.e. consume the Word of God as something to sustain and nourish our hearts, we will grow stronger in the Lord. We will arm ourselves with Scripture and prepare for spiritual warfare. So we must not lose hope, God will provide beauty and remind us of His character, if we only open our eyes to what He has given us.

13

Photosynthesis

*Then Jesus spoke to them again, saying, "I
am the light of the world. He who follows Me
shall not walk in darkness, but have the light
of life.* –John 8:12 NKJV

I remember learning about photosynthesis in the fourth
grade. It sounded so interesting to me. Not only was it a
new, five syllable word, it made me sound smart when I told
my parents what I had learned. We even read a book about a
boy who tried to photosynthesize himself[11]. Obviously, it is a
work of fiction, but it is creative, and it helped my nine-year-
old mind learn the gist of the process. In a very basic sense,
plants absorb sunlight and convert that to energy, helping
them grow and flourish.

I hope you can see where I'm going. God is referred to
as Light throughout the Bible. 1 John 1:5 says, "This is the
message which we have heard from Him and declare to you,
that God is light and in Him is no darkness at all." John 8:12
also tells us, "Then Jesus spoke to them again, saying, "I
am the light of the world. He who follows Me shall not walk
in darkness, but have the light of life". In church language,

we hear the comparison of light and dark all the time. God is light; the world is darkness. Fitting. Like the first verse I shared in 1 John, if we are walking with God, there should be no darkness. I say "should", not "will", because we are sinful people, but that is what we strive for. This verse does assure us that nothing dark can come from God. Any darkness is the result of our own sin.

Our ultimate goal as Christians is to be more and more like Christ every day, and to grow into a beautiful, Jesus follower (hmm…looks a lot like "flower", doesn't it?). When we spend time in the Light, we grow. Photosynthesis! (In the most metaphorical sense, of course.) When we are weary, He lifts us up (2 Corinthians 12:9). Have you ever seen a flower perk up in the sunlight? The flower's face can be pointing toward the dirt, but the sun comes out, and it slowly faces skyward. Or imagine trees that canopy over roads. They follow the sun as it rises on one side and sets on the other, leaving the trees on either side growing toward the light. Galatians 6:9 says "And let us not grow weary while doing good, for in due season we shall reap if we do not lose heart". Just like the plants, His light sustains us and nurtures us. When we feel like we cannot possibly lead worship for one more early service or teach one more kindergartener about Jonah, when we are worn down trying to trudge through Leviticus, God is right there, ready to shine on us and give us energy, renewed strength. He lifts our faces out of the dirt and into His marvelous light.

We cannot do this on our own. Flowers cannot grow without water and light. We can't do it either.

Living Water

> *Jesus answered and said to her, "If you knew the gift of God, and who it is who says to you, 'Give Me a drink,' you would have asked Him,*

71

and He would have given you living water.-
John 4:10 NKJV

Let's take a look at the woman at the well in John chapter 4. She was thirsty in a physical and spiritual sense, although she was only ready to acknowledge her need for a sip of well water. She had obviously struggled with sinful relationships, and Jesus knew this. He lovingly tells her He can offer "living water" (verse 10) that will satisfy her thirst forever. Verses 13-14 say, "Whoever drinks of this water will thirst again, but whoever drinks of the water that I shall give him will never thirst. But the water that I shall give him will become in him a fountain of water springing up into everlasting life". Jesus' water can fill her in a way sin cannot.

Trying to satisfy our needs with sin is like nourishing a flower with Dr. Pepper. Sure, it looks good, and if the flower had taste buds, it would sing a hallelujah or two, but the necessary nutrients would be absent. It would ultimately result in the demise of the flower. We cannot live in sin and grow in Christ. The only way to thrive is to stand in His presence, absorbing His light and his living water.

As a life-long church-goer, this sounds fine and good, but if you are feeling lost with the metaphors, that is okay. Let's review.

God=Light
World=Darkness
People=Flowers
Jesus=Water

When we let God rule our lives, we grow. When we let the world rule our lives, we fail.

The woman at the well was living in darkness. She was looking to men to find her self-worth and her purpose, and coming up short. When Jesus explained He could set her free from that, she knew she was ready for a change. Her face rose from the dirt and to the Son. Plants naturally gravitate toward the things they need. God designed us to do that too, but unfortunately, we get distracted. We gravitate towards the easy fixes and the pretty packaging. God created us to think, but we trust in our own foolish instincts instead of depending on Him. In this way, and many others, we need to "go back to our roots", if you will, and follow the flowers.

Unlike the book I read as a child, we can't photosynthesize ourselves. We don't have the capability to provide our own Light and Water. We must allow God to provide those things for us in order to thrive. It is definitely counterintuitive to the messages we hear today that say we must be self-sufficient, independent, and powerful. Jesus was counterintuitive, though, and we are supposed to be like Him. If the Word is our Water, and God is our Light, I would rather listen to what He says, anyway.

14

Get Outside

So He said, "Come." And when Peter had come down out of the boat, he walked on the water to go to Jesus. –Matthew 14:29

I'm not about to tell a lie. My idea of rest and relaxation involves the couch, a good book, a cup of tea, and some Gilmore Girls. My first thought is not to spend time in the great outdoors, but if I were to spend all of my time inside, I would miss out on a lot of beauty from God. Because God is everywhere, He is very present in my living room. I feel Him when I'm reading my Bible or singing worship songs in my car. But I SEE Him in the sunset, in the waves, and in the mountains. I smell His fragrance in flowers, and I acknowledge His nearness in the breeze. I do not want to sound like a tree-hugger, but I truly appreciate God's presence in nature.

God does not make us work to find Him. He is with us always, just as He promises in Matthew 28:20. However, there is more to a relationship with Christ than simply acknowledging His presence. It is easier to say "Yes, I believe in God" than it is to wake up early to read the Bible or trust

His goodness in the middle of life's storms. We cannot rest in His promises if we don't know what His promises are. God's Word tells us in Jeremiah 29:13 "And you will seek Me and find Me, when you search for Me with all your heart" (NKJV).

What does it mean to seek something with your *whole heart*? Have you ever used the phrases, "I poured my heart into that" or "I love you with all my heart"? Think of what goes behind those statements. When you pour your heart into something, you strive for perfection. You may spend countless hours working on a project to bring it to completion. You make sacrifices to ensure it is done and done well. Loving someone with your whole heart means you choose that person over others. You serve them, you do what you can to please them, you brag about them to other people. Again, you make sacrifices to see that person's needs met. Now apply these actions to your relationship with God. How does it stack up? I will admit, my decks are uneven.

Imagine that this is your relationship with God, though. You truly seek Him with your whole heart. Does that leave you stagnant, in one place, doing the same thing every day? Reading a Psalm a day or a three-minute devotional in the morning? No. It places you "outside", looking for ways to find God in everything. Learning about His character, His goodness, and His promises will not only equip you for trials, it will deepen your relationship with our Creator.

So here is what I mean by "getting outside". Do not let your relationship with God get stale. Pursue Him, knowing He is actively pursuing you, too. Making time with Him each day can seem like a chore at first, but the more you do it, the more you will crave that time. I choose to wake up early each day to read and study His Word. It is not always easy, but it is always worth it. There is not some magical formula to make your day go smoothly because you read your Bible in the morning, but it is never time wasted, and I always leave my quiet time in a better place than when I started.

Being in a relationship with someone you love means you want to spend as much time as possible with them, not just in times of celebration, and certainly not only when you are struggling. So why would our relationship with God be any different? We should be in constant communication with Him throughout the day. When you see something beautiful, praise God for His creation. When you face a near miss situation while driving, thank God for protecting you. When your child is, as my mom would say, "tap dancing on your last nerve", pray for patience and grace. Making God a part of your everyday life and actions will only increase your intimacy with Him.

One of my go-to Bible stories is in Matthew 14:22-33. It is a very well-known story of Jesus walking on the water, and Peter taking a step of faith to follow Jesus' lead. My good friend, Steph, often references this story to encourage others to act in faith by using the phrase, "Get out of the boat!". Peter would not have experienced this amazing feat had he chosen to just sit and watch Jesus. He had to physically trust Jesus to keep him above the water. The miracle happened *outside* the boat.

How many times have you heard the phrase, "get out of your comfort zone"? Why do we encourage others not to play it safe? Because great things can happen when we stretch our limits. I would not even know my job existed had I chosen the easy route in college. As I stated before, I had an internship opportunity available at my existing job, but my professor caught my attention when he urged us to explore options besides the path of least resistance. Nine years later, and I'm so grateful for this professor's wise words.

I have heard dozens of stories of people feeling God's call to do something uncomfortable, like calling an acquaintance out of the blue, or giving money to a stranger, or sharing a testimony, and seeing end results that are life-changing. Someone was ready to commit suicide, until a stranger rang their doorbell for no reason other than God told him to. A single mom had nothing to feed her children, until a woman handed her a grocery store gift card. A teenager asked God for a sign that showed up in the form of an unsuspecting passerby with a word from God. These are not found by sitting on the couch.

God created Adam and Eve outside in a garden. He did not place them in a house or a tent. He gave them a bed of grass and a roof of leaves; he fed them with fruit and quenched their thirst with a river. He gave them the sun for warmth (I'm sure without sunburn before the Fall of Man), trees for shade, birds for music, and His presence forever. I truly believe God has an affinity for nature; He created it, after all. So get outside, figuratively and literally speaking. Explore the creativity, directly from God's own hands. Do something that you have never done before to bring you on a closer walk with Him. Learn the ways God communicates with His people. We only need to listen and look around. Get out of that boat!

15

Sowing Seeds of Discord

Sow for yourselves righteousness; reap in mercy; break up your fallow ground, for it is time to seek the Lord, till He comes and rains righteousness on you. Hosea 10:12

The goal of planting a seed is growth. Planting a sunflower seed will yield a sunflower, planting a zucchini seed with yield zucchini, and so on. Typically, planting a seed is a good thing. Unfortunately, we sometimes plant seeds that cause others harm.

I think the best, well, really the worst, example of this is gossip. When we tell a friend a rumor that has negative connotations toward him or her, we aren't doing anything but adding to the hurt and probably spreading a lie. This is sowing a seed of discord. This is not planting something to thrive and sustain life, this is planting a weed to suffocate the good.

Proverbs 6:16-19 says, "These six things the Lord hates, yes, seven *are* an abomination to Him: A proud look, a lying tongue, hands that shed innocent blood, a heart that devises wicked plans, feet that are swift in running to evil, false witness who speaks lies, and one who sows discord among brethren." These are the things God hates, and sowing discord is right there in black and white, right next to some pretty serious stuff. You know, the "bad" sins, like murder and words like *wicked* and *evil*.

Yet we throw gossip around like confetti, thinking it will make us look better if we have the juicy details. We pick up magazines that have horrible things written about celebrities, who we tend to forget are real people with real feelings. We hear from so-and-so who heard from so-and-so something really terrible about an acquaintance. And instead of praying for that person and the awful situation they are in, we run and tell the next person. Or, we sow the seeds of discord and tell the subject of the rumor exactly what is being said about them, under the guise that you are just trying to be a good friend and let them know what's going on. Now you have created a filthy mix of emotions and messages with little to no validity and stamped your name across it. Can you understand why God hates this? It is confusing, hurtful and without purpose or value.

We gossip to make ourselves look good. We think if we have the latest news, we will be valued. If we have a story of how messed up someone's life is, ours will look better by comparison. But what we need to realize is gossiping says more about the messenger than the subject of the message. If you are sharing one person's secret, you are probably sharing everyone's secret, and you are not proving to be very trustworthy. Even though you think you are looking out for your own interests, you are shooting yourself in the foot. James 3:16 says, "For where envy and self-seeking exist, confusion and every evil thing are there."

Again, God asks us not to do certain things because it is what is best for us. We want to avoid evil and confusion. We should be seeking kindness, encouragement, and service— sowing seeds of righteousness. I love this verse in Hosea:

"Sow for yourselves righteousness; reap in mercy; break up your fallow ground, for it is time to seek the Lord, till He comes and rains righteousness on you." (Hosea 10:12)

If we sow righteousness, we will produce righteousness. Like the verse says, "it is time to seek the Lord", not ourselves.

Sowing seeds of discord can manifest itself in other ways too. It seems our culture has an "us vs. them" mentality. We don't necessarily understand someone who is different, so we become fearful. We don't like being afraid, so we tear down. We take "facts" out of context or stretch them to make others take our side. Just as with gossip, we create confusion and a feeling of discomfort, and it may be rooted in a lie. We have little to base our assumptions on, and we preach like they are hard facts.

The people we are talking about are God's children. He created them with the exact same effort He used to create you. We are no better, no worse. It hurts when someone talks negatively about us, about our family, about our friends. It hurts God when His children are in discord. In Matthew 22:37-40, Jesus told the scribes, "And you shall love the Lord your God with all your heart, with all your soul, with all your mind, and with all your strength.' This is the first commandment. And the second, like it, is this: 'You shall love your neighbor as yourself.' There is no other commandment greater than these." Again, in John 13:34, Jesus told his disciples, "A new commandment I give to you, that you love one another; as I have loved you, that you also love one another." Clearly, He means business with this whole "love your neighbor" idea.

We are not always going to be in agreement. There are people in this world who will reject God until the day they die. It breaks my heart, but it is true. Do not give them a single reason to reject God. Do not hurt your witness with petty gossip or fearful hatred. The result of sowing seeds of discord is a tangled mess. I imagine thorns and briar, with no added beauty from fruit or flowers. Hurtful and dangerous.

Matthew 5:44-46 says, "But I say to you, love your enemies, bless those who curse you, do good to those who hate you, and pray for those who spitefully use you and persecute you, that you may be sons of your Father in heaven; for He makes His sun rise on the evil and on the good, and sends rain on the just and on the unjust. For if you love those who love you, what reward have you?" If we put the effort into building up than we do to tearing down, I think the world would see a huge change. I know it sounds trite and "Pollyanna", but I really believe it. If Jesus felt it was important enough to say eleven times in the New Testament, I would say He meant business, and we would do well to obey.

What are you sowing?

16

Church Planting

But you shall receive power when the Holy Spirit has come upon you; and you shall be witnesses to Me in Jerusalem, and in all Judea and Samaria, and to the end of the earth. –Acts 1:8

I first became aware of the idea of church planting when I was in high school. A large church in our community saw a need in another part of the community and several families began a smaller church to reach that area. Our family became involved when my mom started leading worship at the church plant. I cannot remember if I knew the term "church plant" at the time, but that is what it was.

Since then, I have been involved with several church plants, in college and through a summer missions program I mentioned before. I have learned from each experience, and I have had amazing opportunities to serve. Just like planting crops though, planting churches is hard work.

If you think church is easy, you aren't involved enough. There is a lot of behind the scenes work to make Sunday mornings happen. From scrubbing floors to adjusting mic stands, to changing batteries, and adjusting A/C units, church staff members are busy.

Planting a church requires the members to advertise, look for real estate, build, repair, set up, tear down, decorate, research, fund, create, serve, preach, teach, pray, sing, play music, entertain, babysit, feed, caffeinate, and report, among other tasks.

It is easy to get burned out while planting a church. If we are honest, it's easy to get burned out just working in a church. God must be involved in every step of the way. This means the motive behind the church plant must be God-honoring as well.

We have our pick of the litter when it comes to places of worship. We can choose what time we attend, what day we attend, we can base our church membership on the worship team or the children's ministry. We can watch online; we can attend a small group. We can go to the east campus or the west campus. We can go to the church that is closest, or to the one near the best restaurants. But when we focus on what the church can do for us, we lose sight of how we can serve God. To continue our theme: bloom where you are planted.

When I started college, I became involved in our Baptist Collegiate Ministry (BCM). The director, Steve, advised the freshmen to spend a few weeks attending a couple different churches, but told us not to spend an entire semester shopping around. Find one you like and settle in. The term "get plugged in" was prominent in the church culture. Do not just go to church, be involved. Be held accountable. If you don't stay in a church, your roots will not get a chance to take hold. You are easily broken and weak.

Church plants work best when members are moving to meet a need rather than to settle a score or keep up with the Joneses. Animosity within the church is inevitable, due to our sinful nature, but we can prayerfully rectify a lot of situations without a schism in a congregation. Plants grow in healthy, fertile soil, rather than old, dried up dirt. Your project needs a fighting chance to begin with.

We do not all have the opportunity to go to the ends of the earth to teach the Gospel. But I can assure you, there are unreached people in your community. This is part of the reason for healthy church planting.

In college, my church met in a bar. No, that is not a typo. Barstools, neon lights, and a makeshift stage created our worship atmosphere. Our idea was to bring the church to the people in a town where partying prevailed over praising Jesus. Granted, we were not in the bar during operating hours, but we knew it was a familiar building for a lot of college students. Plus, they didn't charge us rent because we cleaned the bar each Sunday morning. (I told you— I learned a lot!) We had banners and decorations to cover the more "revealing" posters, and we had, on more than one occasion, visitors who were pleasantly surprised to see the bar open on a Sunday, only to feel a little awkward once they realized what was going on. Our location was a fun conversation starter, and we had multiple opportunities for outreach, but it didn't really catch on. Just like some seeds don't take root, our church plant didn't either.

Despite a gardener's best efforts, some seeds just fail to grow. Yet the gardener does not, and must not give up. He doesn't say "because this seed didn't grow, I am never planting again." He learns from it. He tries again. He knows the remnant of a seed will break down to add nutrients to the soil for the next planting. Church planting is very similar.

Any time the Gospel is presented is not wasted. Any time someone makes a valiant effort to spread God's Word is valued. Sometimes God's goals are not goals we can see or understand. Just because we see something as a failure, doesn't mean God is not back stage applauding for a job well done. Planting is an exercise of faith.

When we plant a seed or a church, there are so many factors outside of our control. We cannot control the weather or reliably control pests; we cannot control who attends a service or if people listen to a sermon. What we can do is continue to plant and continue to preach. If we are listening to God's call and following His lead, we cannot fail, from an eternal perspective.

17

Newness of Life

Blessed be the God and Father of our Lord Jesus Christ, who according to His abundant mercy has begotten us again to a living hope through the resurrection of Jesus Christ from the dead. - 1 Peter 1:3

One thing I love about springtime is seeing new flowers and new growth. Spring brings with it a reprieve from the cold winter months and an overall feeling of hope. While the word "change" evokes feelings of fear and resistance, "new" brings with it interest and desire.

Some of my favorite verses talk about Jesus making all things new. Isaiah 43:19 says, "See, I am doing a new thing! Now it springs up; do you not perceive it?

I am making a way in the wilderness and streams in the wasteland" (NIV). God will take our brokenness, our areas of sin and desolation and create something beautiful.

Revelation 21:5 also says, "Then He who sat on the throne said, "Behold, I make all things new."" This concept that the old selves will go away and become something new shows our Savior's mercy and grace.

We are assured in 2 Corinthians 5:17 that "if anyone is in Christ, he is a new creation; old things have passed away; behold, all things have become new". When we mess up, God will set us right again. He lets us have a do-over and move on, instead of wallowing in shame. Again, in Lamentations 3:22-23, the Bible tells us, "Through the Lord's mercies we are not consumed, because His compassions fail not. They are new every morning; Great is Your faithfulness." Every. Single. Morning. His mercies are new. Jesus told us to forgive our neighbor "seventy times seven" (Matthew 18:22), yet He will forgive even more than that, if we just ask. We are made new.

Maybe this is why gardening is so appealing to me. It is a visual representation of newness in Christ. He takes us as seeds, with no beauty and no value in and of ourselves. He places us in the soil we need to thrive, and if we accept His light and water, we will grow into something beautiful that looks to Him. We cannot do any of this on our own; our Master Gardener must provide what we need, and we must accept it.

Every now and then, I feel stale. I feel like I need a few new pictures on the wall of my living room or a new shower curtain in the bathroom to freshen things up a bit. I may want a new dress to wear to church, a new song to listen to while I fold clothes, or maybe I want to get a haircut. Little changes can make a huge difference. Obviously, none of these things are necessary for survival, and moving some furniture around can provide a cheaper option for change if the budget is tight. We tend to crave new.

I love seeing a verse in a way I have never seen it before. Hebrews 4:12 tells us God's word is "alive and active". That tells me that while it never changes, it can continue to teach me no matter how many times I read it. Reading a verse in a new light or a new circumstance can set my heart on fire. It is exciting, as if God has spoken to me, personally, in that very moment. In fact, that is exactly what He has done. I have heard it said that if we want to hear God speak to us, read the Bible out loud. His Word is at our fingertips.

In the church, we often speak of the phrase "born again". As Nicodemus learned in the book of John, chapter 3, we do not reenter our mothers' wombs, but we start afresh. We leave our old lives of sin and start on new journeys toward following Christ at all cost. I often hear Romans 6 quoted in reference to baptism, an act that follows a public profession of faith. "What shall we say then? Shall we continue in sin that grace may abound? Certainly not! How shall we who died to sin live any longer in it? Or do you not know that as many of us as were baptized into Christ Jesus were baptized into His death? Therefore, we were buried with Him through baptism into death, that just as Christ was raised from the dead by the glory of the Father, even so we also should walk in newness of life" (Romans 6:1-4). Basically, we should not continue on the old, sinful paths of life. We press on with the goal of glorifying God in everything we do. We get clean slates. Something new.

At the end of a season of harvest, most crops are pulled up to start over for the next year. Very few continue to produce year after year. This gives the gardener a chance to choose new crops or change the number of plants. It is a fresh start. Gardening is active. As we have discussed, it is hard work. The labor is intense, and it never ends. But the fruits of the labor are literal and abundant. When you reap, you sow. When you choose not to plant seeds, you go without.

This is why the gardening analogy is so applicable to Christianity. When we are faithful to share the gospel and live a life according to our call, we see growth. When we go through the motions and avoid stepping out of our comfort zones, we may never see a harvest.

It's also something we must constantly pursue. One fantastic worship service may carry us for a while, but that emotional high will eventually wear off and leave us craving more. God designed us that way for a reason. He wants us in constant communication with Him. He wants our relationship to be lifelong, not hit and miss. He knows our lives are so much richer when that happens.

I think it is good to crave *new*. Wanting new sends us on journeys to find God in places we might have otherwise missed Him. *New* allows us to start another Bible study or book about faith. *New* puts us on a plane to share the gospel in an impoverished country. *New* takes us out of our comfort zone to leading worship on Sunday morning. We learn to thrive on the thrill of seeing flowers bloom. We grow in our patience as we continue to till soil and water our crops, even when the cultivating season seems eternal. We know from experience that the wait is worth it. Newness will come, and God will refresh us once again. Pursue newness with God.

18

A Bouquet

When you buy flowers, you typically buy more than one. You receive a flower arrangement, or a bouquet. Even if it contains several of the same type of flower, they just look nicer in a bunch. Unless, of course, it's the rose from "Beauty and the Beast". That beauty stands alone.

A florist knows how to put together different types of flowers to complement each other in size, color, and shape. The pink undertones in one petal may bring out a stripe of pink in another flower. A tall bulb may stack nicely next to a shorter one. Branches and leaves may add some texture to the arrangement. Full flowers may make a solid center, while smaller petals fit around the perimeter.

The point is, flowers look best when they are with other flowers. We admire flower beds for the collection of plants and blooms, rather than a single stem growing alone. And just like you have probably guessed, we do better in groups, too. I am sure you have heard it said, there is strength in numbers. We grow more when we are in fellowship with other believers. We are more likely to absorb a sermon when we physically go to church. The accountability we have by surrounding ourselves with other Christians of all ages and walks surpasses a solo lifestyle.

We are designed for relationships; we learn from each other's talents and gifts. We are stronger against the devil when we have another believer holding us up. Ecclesiastes 4:12 tells us, "Though one may be overpowered by another, two can withstand him. And a threefold cord is not quickly broken." Certain flowers are considered "allies" when it comes to gardening. Vegetables rely on different types of flowers to deter bugs and other dangers. Marigold, for instance, repels beetles[12]. This can be especially helpful when trying to grow produce that is susceptible to predators. We need friends like that. We need people who will help us fight off temptation and avoid situations which cause us to stumble.

When planting a vegetable garden, depending on what types of vegetables you having growing next to each other, you can alter the taste. Bell peppers planted next to a jalapeno plant may taste a little spicier than those planted next to tomatoes. My pastor's lemon tree cross-pollinated with his neighbor's orange tree to produce the sweetest lemons I have ever tasted. Again, we become like the people with whom we associate. If we are constantly spending time with someone who worries, we might start to pick up that quality too. We pick up mannerisms and language of those around us, good or bad. When we associate with positive people who encourage and build up those around them, we start to strive for that, too.

Coming together with fellow believers allows for a pool of ideas, a team of prayers, and friends to keep you in check. When I have had a rough day at work or trouble parenting, my friends at Bible study can tell by my face when something is off. It can be so therapeutic to just talk it out for a minute. Once it is unloaded, it is easier to dissipate. When I am struggling with a decision or a problem, having a lot of people praying is such a humbling, awe-inspiring experience.

A garden would not be a garden without an array of flowers and plants or fruits and vegetables. A church would be lacking if we were all good at the same things. We need the various colors, shapes, smells, and heights to construct the beautiful bride of Christ. We feed off each other's strengths and build up each other in weakness. We are grounded in the same soil; our roots grow alongside each other. We can rest in the same foundation of Christ's salvation and live our lives accordingly.

I think the same principle is true in families as well. My two boys are very different, just like my sister, Whitney, and I are like night and day. Whitney is an orchid, while I'm a lily. If my mom had two of me, life might be a little boring. My sister adds a certain flair to life that I just don't have. Together, we balance life well and make a lovely bouquet. I think my mom and dad could vouch for me on that.

We need people with different petals. We need people who thrive in sunlight, but also in the shade. It is important to associate ourselves with people who don't always look like us or think like us. In this process, though, we must remain rooted in Christ. Different can be good and beneficial, but we cannot forget God's Word in the process. Remember Who our Gardener is, and do not let false teaching prevail.

Be a good neighbor. Be a flower that deters the Enemy and welcomes God's presence. Bring out the best in others, and have a fragrance that is pleasing to God. Stand tall when you need to be brave, and lay low when humility is necessary. Look for the good qualities in others, and acknowledge in love when there is room for growth. Remember, God created us to live in harmony with others. Fulfill that destination.

Conclusion

We have the opportunity to serve an amazing God. He is actively involved in our lives. He loves us enough to not only help us grow, but give us everything we need to grow. Our Master Gardener knows what makes us flourish, what encourages us, what causes us pain or fear, and what tools we need to equip us to help others. He has given us beauty beyond belief and Scripture for any and every situation we come across in this life. Above all, He made the ultimate sacrifice of His only Son, in order to secure an eternal life with Him.

You can look all over God's green earth to see what He has orchestrated. From the tiniest of clovers to the most majestic mountain ranges, His creativity is surpassed by no one, and it has the power to take breath away.

The next time you receive a bouquet of flowers or see a plate of fresh produce, take it at more than face value. Thank God for the meaning behind it. Reflect on the soil in which it grew, the seed that started it all, the sun and water that nourished it, and the Creator who designed it to begin with. Think of the hands God equipped to plant it and the time it took to grow. Apply it to your life and see just how God has grown you from a tiny seed to the flourishing person you are today. It is only by God's grace.

For we are but seeds, planted on this earth with purpose, designed to grow and flourish in His creative hands. Apart from Him, we die. In Him, we are part of a garden of His making.

So retreat to a garden- metaphorical or physical- and spend time with God, our Master Gardener. What kind of seed will you be? Set aside time to praise Him, to learn who He is. Be the flower. The tighter the relationship, the more plentiful the produce. Keep your eyes on Him and be nourished. Keep your eyes on Him and see His goodness.

He turns rivers into a wilderness,
And the water springs into dry ground;
A fruitful land into barrenness,
For the wickedness of those who dwell in it.
He turns a wilderness into pools of water,
And dry land into water springs.
There He makes the hungry dwell,
That they may establish a city for a dwelling place,
And sow fields and plant vineyards,
That they may yield a fruitful harvest.
He also blesses them, and they multiply greatly -Psalm 107:33-38

Acknowledgements

Daniel, thank you for being my greatest supporter and encourager. I'm forever thankful for my best friend and partner in this crazy life we live. From blog to book, you've shown excitement and interest in my projects, and you've kept me going. I love you.

Whitney, you're my biggest cheerleader. I can't thank you enough for your belief in me. Thank you for making me laugh more than anyone I know. I larva you, Seester.

Mom, thank you for raising me in a home where Jesus' name was spoken and church was not optional. You planted in me the belief in the power of prayer. And thank you for making sure I didn't overuse "simply". I love you.

Dad, thank you for always being proud of me and making me feel like I could succeed in anything. "Hit 'em straight."

My Oak Grove family, John and Jo, thank you for showing me what it means to be in a relationship with Jesus and teaching me what it is to love Him. You've been a springboard for missions, Bible study, community, and talents. I'm proud to call you family.

Kate M., thank you for sharing a love of all things grammar and for your proofreading skills. There, their, they're.

Endnotes

1   Eden. 2016. In *Merriam-Webster.com*. Retrieved October 1, 2016, from http://www.merriam-webster.com/dictionary/eden
2   Peterson, A. (2010). Planting Trees On *Counting Stars* [CD]. Seattle, WA: Centricity.
3   Bleakley, R., Boyd, A., Comfort, P., Jordan, I., Kernoghan, P., McCann, A. (2008). God of This City on *God of This City* [CD]. Atlanta, GA: sixsteps.
4   BBC News (2013, June 19). RHS 'sheep-eating plant about to bloom in Surrey. *BBC News*. Retrieved from http://www.bbc.com/news/uk-england-surrey-22967160
5   Grazer, B. (Producer), & Reitman, I. (Director). (1990). *Kindergarten Cop* [Motion picture]. USA: Universal Pictures.
6   Miles, C. (1913) In the Garden (Public Domain)
7   Broach, D. (2016, September 15). How Many People, Houses Flooded in Louisiana. *Times-Picayune*. Retrieved from http://www.nola.com/weather/index.ssf/2016/08/how_many_people_houses_were_fl.html
8   http://www.nbcolympics.com/video/divers-johnson-and-boudia-rely-faith-put-minds-ease
9   Covey, S. (1989). *The Seven Habits of Highly Effective People*. New York, NY: Free Press
10 http://www.dictionary.com/browse/worship
11 Gardiner, J.R. (1995). *Top Secret*. U.S.A.: Little, Brown Books for Young Readers
12 (2007). Companion Planting Guide. In *Burpee*. Retrieved from http://www.burpee.com/gardenadvicecenter/areas-of-interest/flower-gardening/companion-planting-guide/article10888.html

Printed in the United States
By Bookmasters